A World of Children's Songs

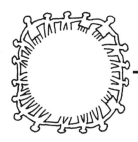

A World of Children's Songs

Edited by Mary Lu Walker

Illustrated by Gloria Ortiz

Friendship Press
New York

Copyright © 1993 by Friendship Press
Editorial Offices:
475 Riverside Drive, New York, NY 10115
Distribution Offices:
P.O. Box 37844, Cincinnati, OH 45222-0844

Manufactured in the United States of America
Printed on recycled paper

Library of Congress Cataloging-in-Publication Data

A World of children's songs / edited by Mary Lu Walker ; illustrated
   by Gloria Ortiz.
     1 score.
     Principally for voice and piano.
     Includes chord symbols.
     Includes bibliographical references.
     ISBN 0-377-00260-7
     1. Children's songs. 2. Folk songs. I. Walker, Mary Lu.
   M1992.W67 1993   93-709103
                                                          CIP
                                                           M

Contents

America South of the Rio Grande 137

Acknowledgments

I wish to thank the following people who helped me find songs or gave me advice about them: Sue Ahn; Vidal Arias; Miss Atlas; Father Kevin Barr; Saroja Chandra; Children's Library, Suva, Fiji; Patrick Colgan; Mitzie Collins; Corning Area Library, Corning, N.Y.; Fenneka Dykeman; Bjorn Eidsvig; Parveen Fard; Paul Glass; Jan Glover; Gazyna Gross; Mamta Hansji; Ian Harrop; Natalya Kara; Nasim Khera; Library, Fiji Broadcasting Co; Vivian Muñoz-Halm and Corning-Painted Post West High School Spanish IV students; Nang Si Si Win; New Zealand Embassy, Suva, Fiji; Pacific Theological College Day Care Center, Suva, Fiji; Kaushe Ratuasara; Rita and Gunars Reimanus; Ray Repp; Dianne Roe; Louis Rossi; Sai Htun Naig Win; Samoan students, Pacific Regional Seminary, Suva, Fiji; Rozanne Shu; Mala Singleton; Mary Knysh Smith; Dr. Rosalie Sneyd; Sun Yat Sen School, Suva, Fiji; Teri Tibbett; Edith Trienan; Judith C. Tucker; UCLA School of Music; UNICEF; Milli Valli; Dr. L.M.S. Van Den Blink; Lana Voituck; Elizabeth Whitehouse; Ray Winieski. Finally, I want especially to thank Don Walker, patient and helpful partner of 41 years.

Preface

When I began work on *A World of Children's Songs*, I gathered material from the hundreds of collections of international folk music published in the United States during the 1950s, 1960s, and 1970s, the golden years of the folk revival in America. I found books containing the printed words and music of people from almost every region on this planet and "read" my way through the shelves of the 780 section of libraries across the country. I was familiar with many of the songs I came across, but I had actually *heard* only a fraction of the thousands that had been captured and preserved on the printed page, many of them like exotic butterflies fixed in resin. In this day of the compact disc and audio cassette, I began to wonder if the world needed yet another book of songs.

In the midst of my research, my husband joined the United Nations as a volunteer and we moved to Suva, Fiji, "the Crossroads of the Pacific." Along with the sunscreen and the mosquito lotion, I packed the unfinished manuscript of this book. Fiji is a developing nation where people from around the world come to live and work. Suddenly, I had "live" resources, and one of the first questions I'd ask a new acquaintance from Tanzania or Korea or the Netherlands was, "Can you sing me a song that every child in your country knows and loves?" I was seldom refused and I was excited to hear songs I'd only "read" before come alive. I loved hearing the sounds of different languages, and my new friends were pleased and eager to help when I tried to stumble along with the lyrics. I found that when I made the effort to learn even a few words in Korean or Swahili or Norwegian, walls crumbled, and music, the universal language, brought us together in an easy and natural way.

The magic combination of rhythm and tune helped me remember unfamiliar speech patterns, and soon I was fearlessly trilling r's and attempting to find my way up and down and in and out of scales foreign to my Western ears. All my "teachers" spoke English to some degree and were able to give me rough translations of their songs; and although I am neither a linguist nor an ethnomusicologist, my understanding of other people grew through the simple act of our singing together. Since American folk and popular songs are known throughout the world, no songfest was ever complete without some of these old favorites sung in the accents of Germany or Thailand or India.

The content of *A World of Children's Songs* was shaped by the "voice on" experiences, which reinforced my conviction that music is the most powerful of teaching tools, a beautifully simple way to help children take the first steps toward understanding cultures different from their own. An American child who learns to sing a song loved by children in Africa or Fiji or Mexico is going to find it easier to realize that Africans and Fijians, Mexicans and Americans, are more alike than different, all members of the human family. I hope the songs in this collection of musical butterflies from around the world will be passed along by dedicated and enthusiastic teachers to a new generation of children, who, if they are to live together in peace on this small planet, must begin to sing together.

Introduction

A World of Children's Songs does not presume to be a definitive collection of songs from every country, although it does contain material from the seven major geographical-cultural regions into which it has somewhat arbitrarily divided the globe. One of its goals is to give children musical windows through which they can see into cultures different from their own. The examples included here, taken as a whole, can tell us much about the world of children wherever they may be. These songs are loved and sung by children because they are about the powerful stuff of life—family, work and celebration, sadness and happiness. The imaginative and adventurous leader or teacher can make use of this musical mortar to cement facts together to add texture and color to a child's understanding of life.

A second, equally important goal of this book is to provide a musical resource that will help teachers, leaders, and parents introduce children to languages other than English. For many American adults, just the sight of a foreign word on the printed page is enough to discourage the use of a song, no matter how good the tune. Afraid of mispronouncing the words or of sounding pretentious if we do say them correctly, we stick to English. Consequently, the extent of most American children's repertoire of songs in another language is limited to "Frère Jacques"; adults don't feel self-conscious singing or teaching those French words because *we* learned them as children. I believe the time has come to move beyond "Frère Jacques" because the simple truth is that children will tackle any language as long as someone takes the time to teach them.

The third goal for *A World of Children's Songs* is to offer songs that are easy to learn and fun to sing. Whether or not one chooses to use them as resource material or teaching tools, the songs in this collection are enjoyable bits of the world's culture that need to be shared with each new generation.

Kinds of Songs

Most of the songs in this collection are folk songs, but there are also some church songs and some secular songs composed by known individuals. Many songs have traveled from their country of origin to other parts of the world. In the old days songs traveled in the memories and voices of living people. Today some songs still move that way, but many are carried by electronic means. As they move, orally transmitted songs change a bit in a new culture, thus blurring the distinction between types of songs.

Folk Songs

By some definitions, a folk song is one of unknown authorship that is passed along from generation to generation in the oral tradition of a culture. Every culture has a heritage of songs that its people just "know" without remembering how or when they first heard them. Such songs may be about food, for example, "Kalina Tree" from Ukraine or "Fruits and Vegetables" from India. There are songs of celebration, such as "Las Mañanitas" from Mexico and "The Butterfly" from Peru; and of course, every culture has its own treasury of lullabies— "Rock-a-bye, Baby Bear" from Latvia is especially appealing. Such songs show how much people are alike all over the world but at the same time highlight their differences. No one knows who composed them; they belong to everyone and to no one.

Many of these folk songs will be old friends, chosen because the tunes will come easily, leaving more time to concentrate on the words. Multilingual versions of "Everybody Loves Saturday Night" and "Jingle Bells" are included for this reason, and the ubiquitous "Frère Jacques" is here with lyrics phonetically interpreted in seven languages—Maori, Fijian, Japanese, Spanish, Latvian, Icelandic, and, of course, French.

Church Songs

Some of the songs in this book were composed in church settings. From the Pacific Theological Seminary in Suva, Fiji, I collected "Jesus Loves Everyone," a little Sunday School chorus that was probably brought to the Pacific by Christian missionaries from the British Isles, who, along with the French and Dutch, profoundly influenced the music of the island people.

In the process of collecting I learned how language and music can work together to overcome fear and disharmony. The seminary is an ecumenical institution whose students come from 15 island countries and whose faculty is drawn from around the world. Many of the seminarians and faculty members have young children who are cared for on the campus during the day at a most unusual kindergarten. On the first day of school, four- and five-year-olds from the Solomon Islands, Samoa, Fiji, Australia, New Zealand, Tahiti, Cook Islands, Papua New Guinea, and other islands in the South Pacific meet for the first time. They do not speak a common language with one another or with the teachers. On that first day, their Fijian teachers begin to sing with them "Jesus Loves Everyone," teaching the song in six different languages. Within days the children are singing together, singing in one another's language, because, as one of the teachers told me, "This is the way we bring them together, make them understand one another." In this kindergarten, a microcosm of cultures, music becomes a bridge between chaos and order. And it's not just the tune that is important; it is the language, the mysterious and wonderful experience of communication in another person's tongue.

A few years ago I took part in an ecumenical conference of Christian leaders from churches around the South Pacific. The 300 delegates were dignified and powerful adults who represented the spectrum of church leadership—liberal and conservative, powerful urban church and little church in the bush. Several times when discussions became heated and tempers ran high, the presiding secretary, a bishop from Papua New Guinea, would pound the gavel and say, "Let's sing a chorus!" Without further ado, he would break into song, and his favorite was "We Are One Big Happy Family." By the end of a few stanzas, the words seemed true. The lyrics are not complex and the tune is simple, but I think it is a powerful song because it brings people together. My Hindu and Muslim friends like to sing it and teach it to their children.

Composed Songs

Songs written by specific individuals tend to be more recent than folk songs and not to have a regional style. "Garden Song" by Dave Mallet and "Share a Little Bit of Your Love" by Ray Repp are examples of songs by contemporary American composers that are known and loved by children in many developing countries. When songs are orally transmitted to another part of the world, they may, like a folk song, take on some characteristics of the local culture. I once heard a song written by a Russian boy during the Cold War (sometimes called "The Soviet Children's Peace Song") sung by a group of children in a village deep in the interior of one of the Fiji Islands. The tune had been changed just a little, and the pronunciation of the words had been adjusted to fit the local dialect; but the essence of the song was there, and it was plain to see that the children understood what the song meant. When I asked how a Russian song had found its way to this remote spot, I was told that a volunteer worker from the United States had spent a few months in the village and had taught the song to the children. The song has become a part of the culture of Namosi village and will be passed along to future generations by oral tradition, not just the way the composer wrote it but changed in subtle ways to become a Fijian song.

Tips on Usage

A few words on the languages of the lyrics, the cultural context, and the musical arrangements will make this book easier to use.

Languages

All songs in a foreign language except those that consist of nonsense syllables have been provided with an English translation. It is printed on the first line beneath the music. Special care has been taken to make the lyrics singable as well as true to the spirit of the originals. A few words have been changed here and there because of the importance of inclusive language.

Directly under the English line most of the foreign songs have at least one stanza spelled as it is pronounced in the original language or transliterated if the original language does not use the Roman alphabet. Below that line is the original language if it is in the Roman alphabet. A few songs appear only in an English version, for example, "Fruits and Vegetables," "Today Is Eid!" and "Diwali." They were chosen because the lyrics give a colorful word picture of another culture.

For the most successful singing in a non-English language, these suggestions may be helpful: (1) Choose only a song that you are really enthusiastic about. Learn the tune well before attempting the words. (2) Don't worry too much about getting the pronunciation perfect. Just do your best. I remember a wonderful Girl Scout leader in Atlanta, more than 50 years ago, who taught my sister Scouts and me to sing a little French game song about passing a shoe around a circle. I'm sure those French words were colored with a rich North Georgia accent, but I've never forgotten her or the song or the great sense of accomplishment I felt at being able to sing *in French*. But if the thought of learning every foreign word is too daunting, pick out one or two words to sing in the original and sing the rest in English, making sure that you explain the meaning of the foreign phrases or words to the children. (3) If in your community you can find someone from the culture from which the song comes, you might ask for help with pronunciation. Better yet, you could ask such a person to enrich your knowledge of his or her culture or even teach you another song.

The Song as a Window to Another Culture

I've always believed that the right song can be used to teach language or social studies or religion or values or just about any subject you can think of. For example, the Polish "Haying Song" describes all the tasks involved in growing, harvesting, and selling hay. The lyrics can be used to stimulate discussion. Where do the Poles live? Why do they grow hay? Do they still grow hay this way? How is hay harvested in the United States? Do children in the United States work in the fields?

Most songs are introduced with a bit of cultural background. You can convey this material to the children or you may want to skip it and just sing the songs for the sheer pleasure of it. These songs can stand on their own two feet, purely to give enjoyment, but they can also serve by adding to our cultural understanding.

Musical Arrangements

The arrangers have tried to stay as close as possible to the original version of the music. In some instances we have simplified rhythm and melody in order to make the songs easier to sing and to play, yet at the same time we have retained the flavor of the original. For example, in transcribing songs from India, we did not attempt to reproduce every note but "rounded off the edges" because the distinctive sound and rhythm of Indian music are extremely difficult for our Western ears to duplicate.

For many songs, such as "A Kapasule" from Angola, the beat is as important as the melody or the lyrics. In many cultures, the rhythm of clapping hands or sticks might be the only accompaniment to the voice. The Fijian song "Little Heron" (*Na Belo*) is usually sung to the beat of the *lali* drum, but I've seen children use two pencils or even two index fingers to snap out the rhythm on a table or the floor. There is no way to approximate the feeling of drums on the printed page, but libraries often have recordings of music from other cultures that you can borrow. Listening to a good recording of Native American music will make you feel more comfortable about giving a song like "Making Maple Suger" a try. The chords shown with the songs are only suggestions to use with any instrument— keyboard or stringed.

Why Another Song Book?

In an electronic variation of the oral tradition, today's children learn songs by radio, television, video and audio cassettes, and compact discs. Children in Sydney and Amsterdam and Tapei can share the same program that keeps a little boy or girl glued to a television set in Pittsburgh or Los Angeles or London. Even the people in remote villages in the developing world have access to VCR's; and for better or worse, little Jonni and Mere in Namosi, Fiji, watch the same cartoons and music videos as little Jean and Marie in Nancy, France. Why, in this day of electronic communication, do we need more songs on the printed page? Why couldn't they be electronically captured and beamed all over the world? Perhaps they could, but that isn't happening. Even if such electronic bards existed, no image on a screen or sound on a tape can ever take the place of the genuine live singer of songs, and no televised "happening" can ever make people feel as downright happy as they do when they sing together. The songs I've chosen for *A World of Children's Songs* are here to be sung, out loud, and with love and joy. I hope that you'll do just that.

# Asia East of the Caspian

Nearly 3 billion people in 49 countries live in Asia. Much of their music sounds strange to Western ears, partly because Asian scales have different numbers of notes and different sizes of intervals from Western scales, and partly because melody is emphasized supported by rhythm but not by harmony. The music of southwestern Asia, which is predominantly Islamic in culture, will be discussed in the section on the Middle East. In this section we will talk about the music of the Indian peninsula, southeastern Asia, and the Far East.

The music of India is one of the oldest in the world. Hindus believe that it is a gift from God to humans. For centuries, chanting has been an important part of Hindu religious ceremonies. Since Indian music, like most Asian music, has no written tradition, classical musical knowledge has been passed from one generation of musicians to another by revered teachers. The Indian scale has 22 notes, many of which would be found "in the cracks" between the keys of a Western piano. These unfamiliar sounds and the fact that songs have no definite beginnings and endings make classical Indian music very difficult for Westerners to understand and perform. Indian music students themselves may study for months before perfecting even one *tala* (rhythm pattern) or learning one *raga* (complicated melody pattern). A folk tradition of less complicated music exists in India just as it does in Western countries. It is usually concerned with aspects of daily life—harvest, fishing, animals, and, of course, love.

The music of southeastern Asia is influenced by that of India, but other countries have left their mark. For example, the folk songs of Sri Lanka (formerly Ceylon) often reflect in their melodies the music of the Portuguese, Dutch, and English who ruled the country at different times. The music of Myanmar (formerly Burma) and of Cambodia has each its own character but shows the influence of China, which has been a dominant economic and political force in that area.

The Chinese believed that musical sounds have magical and divine power and that it is important to sing or play with proper expression and tone. Each season—spring, summer, autumn, and winter—is interpreted musically by a special pitch and series of notes. In contrast to the Indian scale of 22 notes, Chinese music is based on the pentatonic (5-note) scale, which corresponds to the black keys on the piano. The melody almost takes its shape from the lyrics because the meaning of Chinese words changes according to the tone in which they are spoken. Instruments include zithers, lutes, dulcimers, oboes, flutes, and fiddles. Singing, whether operatic song or folk song, is in a nasal style that sounds harsh to Western ears.

Korean music, like other aspects of Korean culture, is a blend of Chinese influence and Korean tradition. Some of the music performed today is almost 900 years old. Korean music, like Chinese, is often based on the pentatonic scale. Some of the most beloved songs, such as "Bluebird," use waltz rhythm. It is hard to transcribe Korean notation into Western notation because the notes are not always sung or played as written but vary depending on the performer's interpretation. In a folk ensemble, each musician plays his own version of the melody. One of the most important instruments is the oboe. Some types of oboe are so loud they can only be played outdoors. Other instruments are cymbals, flutes, fiddles, and zithers. Two unusual instruments of Chinese origin are a set of 16 chromatically tuned bells (*p'yonjong*) and a matching set of 16 stone slabs (*p'-on-gyong*) pitched an octave higher, which are always played together. Folk music is usually sung by a soloist and accompanied by drums. Drummers also play farmers' music for dancers in long, ribbon-decked hats celebrating the rice harvest.

Japan's traditional songs are also based on the pentatonic scale. The complicated rhythm patterns produced by either hand clapping or a wide variety of percussion instruments make Japanese music distinctive and exciting. Music is an important part of the many festivals that celebrate the seasons or religious holidays. Japanese children love to sing together, and composers are encouraged to write for them. Many children's songs are about animals, insects, family vacations, or games, as well as about the proper way to behave! The songs are melodic and fun to sing. As well as Japanese songs, most Japanese children know Mother Goose nursery rhymes. For years, the songs of the American composer Stephen Foster were favorites in Japanese schools, where they were used to teach English.

In all the big cities of Asia today, and even in small villages, Western influence is strong, but a traditional musical heritage gives a unique and subtle flavor to the new Asian music that is developing.

Diwali
Festival of Lights

Diwali ("festival of lights") is a lovely Hindu celebration that takes place in the month of October. A few weeks before, people gather to dance in honor of Lakshmi (Laxmi), the goddess of wealth. Young girls dressed in their finest saris whirl and dip to the music of drums and flutes. On the day of *Diwali*, houses and yards are lit up with thousands of lights (*diwa*, or little oil lamps made of clay) or strings of electric lights. Neighbors visit one another's houses bringing gifts of sweets. Fireworks light up the night sky.

Words by Mary Lu Walker

Hindu melody
Arranged by Nylea L. Butler-Moore

TABLA or SMALL HAND DRUM

BHAYA or LARGE HAND DRUM

Fruits and Vegetables

Fruits and vegetables make up a good portion of an Indian child's diet, especially in the many Hindu families that are vegetarian. The words to this song paint a picture of the tropical foods available in an Indian market. It is sung in recitative style, traditionally by a girl with a basket on her head.

From the *Marati* of Kashinath Jogdand
English words by Clara L. Seiler

Traditional melody
Notation by Emily R. Bissell

2. Pineapples, pomelos, sweet limes and oranges!
   Pomegranates, too! Who?

3. Bull's hearts, custard apples, please come, and taste my guavas!
   Fruit, vegetables, come, buy! Aye!

Shawl Weaver's Song

In the mountainous region of Kashmir, in northern India, goats produce an especially soft wool. It is woven into light, warm shawls with intricate, richly colored designs. This is a dreamy song a weaver might sing, working long hours at the loom, to make a shawl to keep some mother warm.

Words by Seymour Barnard

Traditional Kashmiri melody

Deft-ly, deft-ly, nim-ble fin-gers, Weave gold and a-zure strands.

Has-ten, has-ten, he who lin-gers, Fly, firm and fa-cile hands.

Weave for moth-er's shoul-der Shawls gay with glint of gold;

For her when bent and old-er, Warm wool a-gainst the cold.

Orange Tree
Me Gase Boho

The people of Sri Lanka will tell you that the sweetest oranges in the world come from their country. When little children sing this song, they praise the orange tree while learning something about sharing with others.

Traditional Sinhalese words
English version by Mary Lu Walker

Traditional melody
Arranged by Nylea L. Butler-Moore

Or - ange tree bends low. Branch - es are
May gah - say boh - hoh. Pah - nee - doh -
Mé ga - sé bo - ho Pa - ni - do -

touch - ing the ground. Plen - ty of or - ang - es,
dah - ahm thee - bay. Pah - heel - ah Ee - deel - ah
dam ___ Thi - bé Pa - hil - a I - dil - a

Sweet, juic - y or - ang - es, or - ang - es all a - round.
Bee - mah - tah Nah - meel - ah Bah - rah-veel ah ah - too.
Bi - ma - ta Na - mil - a Ba - ra - vel - á A - thu.

2. I'll pick one for you
   And you can pick one for me
   Plenty for us to share
   With children everywhere
   From the sweet orange tree.

English version © 1993 by Mary Lu Walker.

Waso
Myanmar July Festival

Waso (pronounced "wahzoh") is the name of a joyous festival in honor of Buddha. It is celebrated in Myanmar (formerly Burma) in the month of July after the rainy season has ended. Children go by bullock carts decorated with flowers into the countryside to pick wild flowers. Their parents tell them, *"Waso pan khu htwet ya aung,"* which means "Come children, we'll go to collect flowers for Buddha."

Words by Mary Lu Walker

Traditional melody
Arranged by Marguerite Clayton

E - ven when the sky is gray, rain - ing, rain - ing ev - 'ry day,

We are hap - py for we know, rain will make the flow - ers grow.

When the sun comes out the chil - dren cel - e - brate with dance and song.

Bud - dha smiles on all the chil - dren. Clouds and rain are gone.

Today Is Your Day
Phleng Wan Koet

This is a traditional Thai birthday song. It sounds better sung in Thai, so we have printed the sound of the Thai words in the Roman alphabet. The little circles and plus signs above the music represent the sounds of a Thai percussion instrument: a circle for an open sound *(ching)* and a plus for a stronger accented beat *(chap)*.

Thai words by Khunying Somrot Sawatdikun
English version by Mary Lu Walker

Melody from Lao Duang Duan
Arranged by Nylea L. Butler-Moore

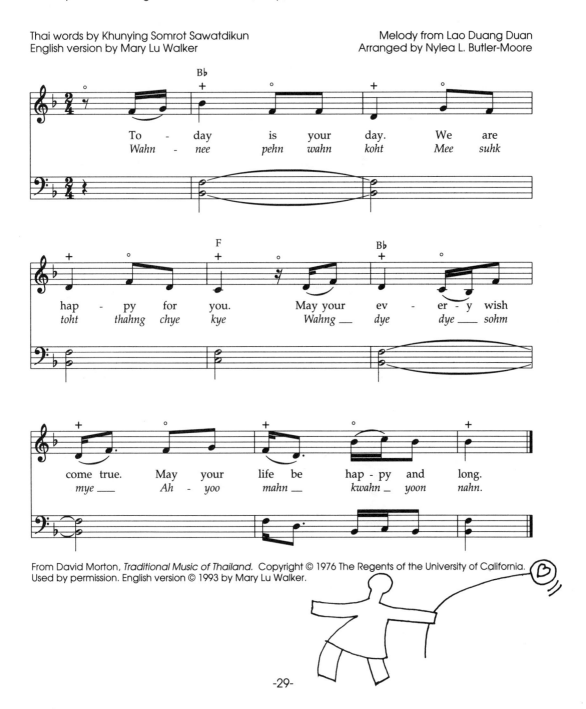

Yangtze Boatmen's Chantey

This traditional work song is popular with the men who pull boats going upstream against the current on the mighty Yangtze River. In rain or shine, cold or heat, the boatmen heave to the rhythm of the chant.

Traditional words
English version by Bliss Wiant

Traditional melody

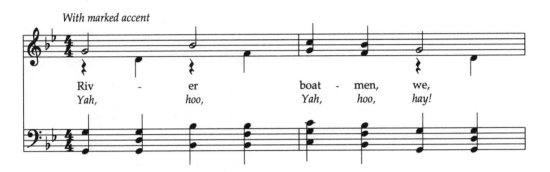

Riv - er   boat - men, we,
Yah,   hoo,   Yah, hoo, hay!

Toil - ing   night and day.   Backs   bend - ing,
Yah,   hoo,   Yah, hoo, hay!   Yye,   yye, yye,

Ropes   tight' - ning,   Sing   we   loud   our   lay.
Hye,   yye, yye,   Yah,   hoo,   Yah,   hoo,   hay!

The Laughing Song
Wah-hah-hah

The original Chinese words to this song describe China as a garden and compare children to flowers in that garden. "Hand in hand we go to the garden where the children are happy and laughing." *Wah-hah-hah* is the sound of laughter. It is hard to sing the song without smiling. The second stanza gives the pronunciation of the numbers 1 to 10 in a Chinese dialect. It can be used to teach children to count.

Words by Mary Lu Walker   Traditional melody

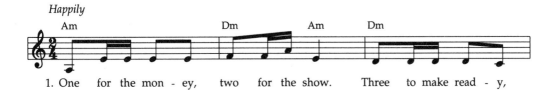

1. One for the mon-ey, two for the show. Three to make read-y,

and four to go! Jump on the bus and we'll all take a ride

out of the ci-ty to the coun-try-side. Wah-hah-hah-ah-ah!

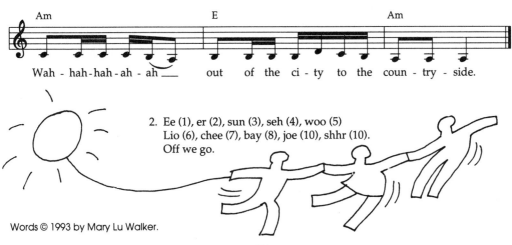

Wah-hah-hah-ah-ah out of the ci-ty to the coun-try-side.

2. Ee (1), er (2), sun (3), seh (4), woo (5)
   Lio (6), chee (7), bay (8), joe (10), shhr (10).
   Off we go.

Frogs

This song from Szechwan Province is a good example of a song using the pentatonic scale. It can be sung as a round. It can also be used to teach children how to multiply — "Two frogs have two mouths. Have four eyes and eight legs. Three frogs have three mouths. Have six eyes and twelve legs," and so on. We have used the pin-yin transliteration system, which approximates the Chinese sounds.

Traditional Chinese words   Traditional melody

In Betty Warner Deitz and T. C. Park, *Folk Songs of China, Japan, and Korea* (John Day Co., 1964).

All by Myself
San Toki

Everyone in Korea loves this song about a rabbit that runs, hops, and fills baskets of chestnuts to give away. *San* means "mountain." *Toki* means "rabbit." It is often sung with motions. In stanza 1 on line 1, put hands on head to resemble ears. On line 3, hop about like a rabbit. In stanza 2 on line 1, walk boldly, swinging arms. On line 3, put chestnuts in mouth. On line 4 walk in reverse direction.

Traditional Korean words
English words by Alma L. Grubbs

Traditional folk melody
Arranged by Allen Tuten

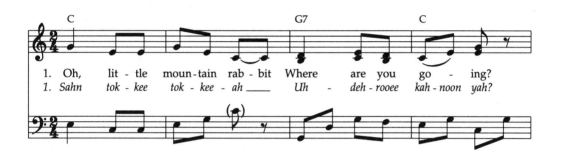

1. Oh, lit-tle moun-tain rab-bit Where are you go - ing?
1. Sahn tok-kee tok-kee-ah ___ Uh - deh-rooee kah-noon yah?

Jump-ing, jump-ing, run-ning so, Where are you go - ing?
Kang-choon, kang-choon dway-myoon-suh, Uh - deh-rool kah-noon-yah!

2. All by myself I'll go
   Over that mountain,
   Gather plump, sweet chestnuts
   Then I'll come back again.

2. *Sahn koh-geh, koh-geh-rooee*
   Nah hon-jah nuh-muh-suh
   Toh-sheel, toh-sheel pahm toh-sheel
   Joo-uh-suh, ohl teh yah!

Used by permission of Alma L. Grubbs.

Doraji

This is a favorite children's folk song. The *doraji* is the Chinese bellflower with purple and white blossoms and edible roots. Korean children love to go into the hills to collect the *doraji*.

English words by Alma L. Grubbs

Traditional melody
Arranged by Nylea L. Butler-Moore

Do - ra - ji pur - ple and __ white, you are good to eat,

beau - ti - ful moun - tain __ top __ do - ra - ji

flow'r. I'll put your sprouts in my __ bas - ket, __

I'll put your flow - ers all in my hair and then __ you will

2. Soon we must go, but we will come gather more to eat.
   One by one, who can find some more, *doraji* sweet?
   Lay the sprouts carefully here in the basket.
   Who can go find a larger flower, a white *doraji*?
   Eh-heh-yah, eh-heh-yah, eh-heh-ee-yah
   Carefully we dig you up, *doraji* sweet.
   Then with seasoned sprouts we put all on our grandpa's table to eat.

Blue Bird
Parangsai

Koreans of all ages love this song about how farmers long ago made jelly from the Indian green bean plant. It is said to be the oldest folk song known in Korea today, more than 1,000 years old.

Traditional Korean words

Traditional melody
Arranged by Nylea L. Butler-Moore

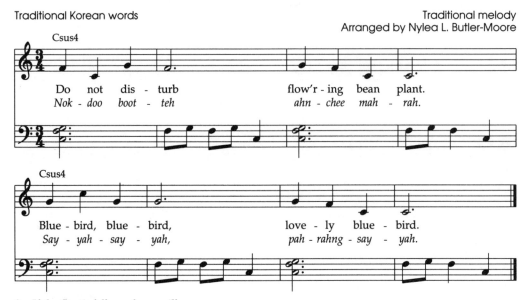

Do not dis - turb   flow'r - ing bean plant.
Nok - doo boot - teh   ahn - chee mah - rah.

Blue - bird, blue - bird,   love - ly blue - bird.
Say - yah - say - yah,   pah - rahng - say - yah.

2. If the flow'r falls, no bean will grow.
   Jelly maker'll go home in tears.

In Betty Warner Dietz and T. C. Park, *Folk Songs of China, Japan, and Korea* (John Day Co., 1964).

Kaeru no Uta
Song of the Frogs

No English words are needed for this Japanese round. The words imitate the sound of a pondful of big and little frogs.

Traditional Japanese words

Traditional melody

Kah eh roo noh   oo tah gah   Kee koh eh teh   koo oo yoh

Kwah kwah kwah kwah   Keh keh keh keh keh keh keh keh kwah kwah kwah.

Sakura

The Japanese people love the flowering cherry tree *(sakura)*, which is a traditional symbol of Japanese culture. Festivals to celebrate the blossoming are held each year throughout the country, and hourly radio and television broadcasts report the opening of the flowers. In spring and early summer on vacation breaks whole schools of Japanese children, marching in school uniform, travel together to see the cherry blossoms or some other notable sight. "Sakura" is a famous poem about cherry blossoms that has been set to music. It is one of the first songs that is played on the *koto,* a stringed instrument. This arrangement is based on an actual performance.

"Sakura"
English words by Katherine F. Rohrbough

Traditional melody
Arranged by Nylea L. Butler-Moore

Cher - ry trees, cher - ry trees bloom so bright in
Sah - koo - rah, sah - koo - rah, yah yoh ee noh

A - pril _ breeze. Like a mist or float - ing _ cloud,
soh rah _ wah. Mee wah tah soo kah guee _ ree,

fra - grance fills the air a - round. Shad - ows flit a - long the _ ground.
kah soo ree kah? koo - moh - kah? Nee oh ee zoh ee zoo _ roo,

Come, oh, come. Come, oh, come. Come see cher - ry trees.
Ee zah yah. Ee zah yah. Mee nee yoo _ kah - n.

Used by permission of Katherine F. Rohrbough.

# M iddle East

The three chief peoples of the Middle East—Arabs, Iranians, and Turks—share a common religion, Islam, which began in Arabia, and a common musical heritage. Middle Eastern music, from northern Africa across southwestern Asia, whether classical, folk, or popular, has a distinctive sound characterized by several instruments playing different versions of the same melody simultaneously. Each instrument is heard individually, rather than their blending into one orchestral sound as in Western music, and there is no attempt at harmony. The scale is made up of whole, half, three-quarter, and five-quarter tones. The chief instruments are lutes (*ouds*) of different kinds in different areas, zithers, flutes, drums, and tambourines.

Arabs tend to emphasize the solo voice. Iranians pay more attention to instrumental music. Turks give equal weight to voice and instrument. Performances can alternate between vocal and instrumental, composed and improvised, solo and group. The texts of songs usually come from classical poetry and are often about love. In Syria, a form of composition called the *waslé* is popular. The singer begins in classical Arabic, moves to a section sung in the dialect of desert dwellers, and ends with a lighter piece in still another dialect. The singer must know three languages and be able to use the voice in different ways to express the words. Folk songs are about the same basic things people sing about everywhere.

In the late 1940s, after World War II, Jewish people from Europe and other nations settled in the newly formed state of

Israel in Palestine. They brought with them their musical traditions, adding yet other voices to the music of the Middle East.

Traditional Jewish music included religious chants for use in the synagogue, based on biblical texts and sung by men without instrumental accompaniment. Later, in the 19th and 20th centuries, it adopted Western influences such as mixed choirs and organ music. Folk songs celebrated the Sabbath, religious holidays, weddings, and events of daily life. "It's Shavuot" and "Hanukkah" are examples. The folk songs of Jews in Germany and eastern Europe showed the influence of local Christian folk tunes. In the Middle East and especially modern Israel, Jewish folk tunes reflect the influence of Arabic music.

Today Is Eid!
Eid Ka Din Ha

In every part of the world, Muslims celebrate *Eid* (pronounced "eed") at the conclusion of *Ramadan,* a 30-day period of fasting that devout Muslims observe each year. The exact date depends on when the first new moon is sighted after *Ramadan.* People light up their houses, and women cook special dishes for their family and friends. A traditional and delicious sweet dish is *sewai,* made with milk and vermicelli noodles. *Eid Ka Din Ha,* which serves as a refrain, means "The Day of Rejoicing."

If you use the optional percussion (see below), notice that these rhythms are in 3/4 time, while the melody is in 4/4 time. The rhythms must be played precisely, not giving in to 4/4 time to accommodate the melody. The *tabla* is the higher-pitched Indian drum. The *bhaya* is the lower-pitched drum. Use a flute or recorder to double the melody.

English words by Mary Lu Walker

Traditional melody
Arranged by Nylea L. Butler-Moore

Who Made Them?
Kis Nay Banaya

Although Pakistan is predominantly Muslim, this song can be sung by children of all faiths since *Kuda* (pronounced "koo-dah") means "God" in Urdu. As Pakistani children sing this song they make appropriate hand motions to suggest fishes swimming, birds flying, flowers, butterflies, and children.

Author of Urdu words unknown
English version by Mary Lu Walker

Traditional melody

2. Who made the birds that fly so high?
   Kis-eh nay bah-neye-ah cheer-ee-yah koh?

3. Who made the flowers that smell so sweet?
   Kis-eh nay bah-neye-ah pool-koh?

4. Who made the pretty butterfly?
   Kis-eh nay bah-neye-ah tit-er-lee koh?

5. Who made all the children here?
   Kis-eh nay bah-neye-ah hum sub koh?

My Ball
Yeh Toop Dooram

For a child who lived 50 or 60 years ago, a simple rubber ball was as cherished a toy as any of the plastic and metal electronic marvels that fill the shelves of stores today. Iranian children still learn this old chant while sitting in the lap of a parent or grandparent, who moves the child's arms in rolling, bouncing, or flying motions to illustrate the words (sort of a Persian "pat-a-cake, pat-a-cake, baker's man"). The words are an approximation of Persian pronunciation. *Toop* means "ball." *Koochooloo* means "little."

Traditional Persian words
English version by Mary Lu Walker

Traditional melody

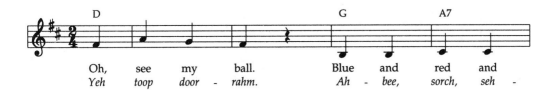

Oh, see my ball. Blue and red and
Yeh toop door - rahm. Ah - bee, sorch, seh -

white. My own lit - tle ball,
feed. Meez - ah - nahm zah meen,

with me day and night. Roll - ing,
hah - vah - mee ___ reh. Gehl - gehl -

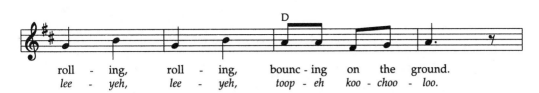

roll - ing, roll - ing, bounc - ing on the ground.
lee - yeh, lee - yeh, toop - eh koo - choo - loo.

Fly - ing up in - to the sky then float - ing down.
Ghel - ghel - lee - yeh, ghel - ghel - lee - yeh toop door - ahm.

Uskudar

This happy folk song is about two lovers on the road to Uskudar (today a suburb of Istanbul). Sing it quickly and rhythmically; don't worry if you can't fit in all the little notes. The Turkish words aren't as difficult as they seem at first glance; take a little extra time to learn them.

Traditional Turkish words
English words by Charles Haywood

Traditional folk melody
Arranged by Allen Tuten

1. As I walked _ one _ rain-y morn' The road to _ Us-ku-dar,
Oos - koo-dar ah gee - der _ ee-kehn ahl - duh-dah beer yah - muhr,
Üs - kü-dar' a gi - der _ i ken al - di-da bir yag - mur,

There I saw my dear _ be - lov - ed,
Kah - tee-bee-mihn say - tray-see oo - zoon
Ka - ti-bi - min se - tre-si u - zun

[1.] Com - ing _ from _ a - far.
ay - tay - ee _ chah - muhr.
e - te - gi _ ça - mur.

[2.] Com - ing _ from _ a - far.
ay - tay - ee _ chah - muhr.
e - te - gi _ ça - mur.

2. On that road I later found
   A kerchief of finest cloth,
   Cleaning it with tend'rest care,
   Surely 'twas his, I thought.

3. Anxiously I looked for him,
   When he appeared near me;
   Promising to wander no more,
   Mine he'll forever be.

In Charles Haywood, *Folk Songs of the World* (John Day Co., 1966).

Tumba

Some say this round comes from Palestine, others that it originated in Russia. Wherever it came from, it makes us think of people dancing and having a good time. *Tumba* (pronounced "toom'-bah") is a nonsense word.

Traditional melody

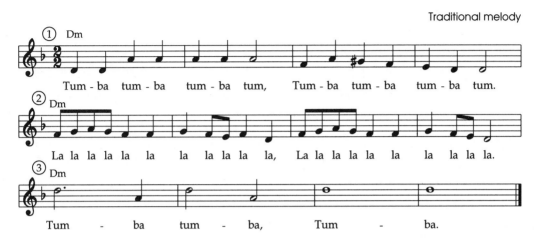

Tum - ba tum - ba tum - ba tum, Tum - ba tum - ba tum - ba tum.

La la la la la la la la la la la, La la la la la la la la la la.

Tum - ba tum - ba, Tum - ba.

Tafta Hindi

Indian fabrics are noted for their high quality; Indian muslin is said to be the finest in the world. In this Arabic folk song (also called Bafta Hindi) a street vendor's calls are supposed to entice women customers, traditionally restricted to their houses, to ask him inside to show his wares.

English words by Louise Barker

Traditional folk melody

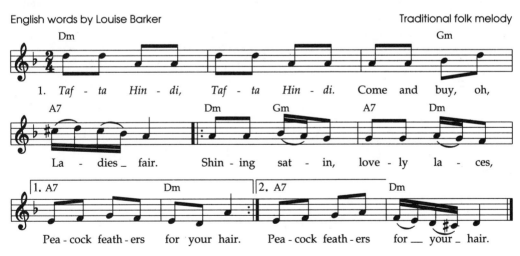

1. Taf - ta Hin - di, Taf - ta Hin - di. Come and buy, oh, La - dies _ fair. Shin - ing sat - in, love - ly la - ces, Pea - cock feath - ers for your hair. Pea - cock feath - ers for _ your _ hair.

2. *Tafta Hindi, Tafta Hindi.*
   Dark eyes peek through silken veil.
   Finger waving, voices calling,
   Bring inside your goods for sale.

3. *Tafta Hindi, Tafta Hindi*
   Come and buy, oh little maid!
   I want satin, I want laces,
   Mother, please buy rich brocade.

A Ram Sam Sam

This song can be sung as a two-part round. The Arabic words have no meaning; they're just fun to sing, with lots of energy and spirit.

Traditional folk melody

A ram sam sam, A ram sam sam, Gu-li, gu-li, gu-li, gu-li, gu-li, Ram sam sam.

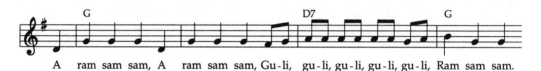

A ram sam sam, A ram sam sam, Gu-li, gu-li, gu-li, gu-li, gu-li, Ram sam sam.

A ra - fi, a ra - fi, Gu-li, gu-li, gu-li, gu-li, gu-li, Ram sam sam.

A ra - fi, a ra - fi, Gu-li, gu-li, gu-li, gu-li, gu-li, Ram sam sam.

In Charles Haywood, *Folk Songs of the World* (John Day Co., 1966).

Hanukkah

In December the Jews keep a very ancient celebration known as Hanukkah, or the Feast of Lights. It commemorates the purification of the Temple in Jerusalem in 165 B.C. after invading Syrians tried to make the Jews worship Syrian gods there. At Hanukkah, candles in a special candlestick, the menorah, are burned for eight days in synagogues and homes. People enjoy parties at which they give presents and play a special game with a *dreidel,* or top. You can find that game described in a companion volume to this one, *A World of Children's Games.*

Translated from the Hebrew of L. Kipnis
by Rabbi Jerome R. Malino

Traditional melody
Arranged by Edith Lovell Thomas

1. Ha-nuk-kah, ha-nuk-kah, fes-ti-val of fun, Light, so soft, shine a-loft joy for ev-'ry-one. Ha-nuk-kah, ha-nuk-kah, tops spin mer-ri-ly, Spin, spin, spin, spin, spin, spin, gai-ly as can be.

2. Hanukkah, hanukkah, lights burn everywhere.
   Pancake treat, cakes to eat, every home will share.
   Hanukkah, hanukkah, happy holiday,
   Let us play, let us sing, let us dance away!

Words used by permission of the translator.

It's Shavuot
Hag Shavuot

Shavuot, or the "Feast of Weeks," is a Jewish feast day held usually in May. In ancient times it was an agricultural festival. It came also to mark God's giving the stone tablets bearing the Ten Commandments to Moses on Mt. Sinai. Sometimes it is accompanied by a dance in a circle. The Hebrew words use the modern transliteration system.

Traditional Hebrew words
English words by Judith Cook Tucker

Traditional melody
Arranged by Allen Tuten
Based on Judith Cook Tucker

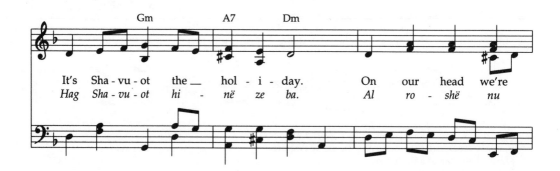

Optional percussion:

TAMBOURINE

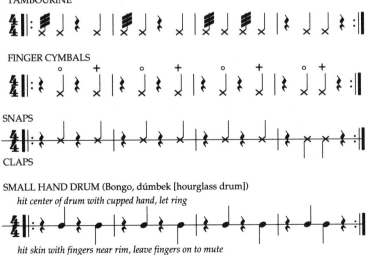

FINGER CYMBALS

SNAPS

CLAPS

SMALL HAND DRUM (Bongo, dúmbek [hourglass drum])

hit center of drum with cupped hand, let ring

hit skin with fingers near rim, leave fingers on to mute

Who Knows One?
Ehad Mi Yode'a?

Every year in the spring Jews all over the world gather in their homes to celebrate Passover at a ceremonial feast, or Seder. They sing and pray from the Haggadah, which tells the story of the ancient Hebrews' miraculous Exodus from captivity in Egypt. The 13 stanzas give the answers to the 13 questions a Jewish boy must know when he is 13 and ready to take an adult's part in religious life. They are in the form of a cumulative song. The Hebrew words are sung to many different tunes depending on a family's musical traditions. This tune was probably sung first in Germany about 1500.

Traditional Hebrew words
English words from *The Songs We Sing*
  by Harry Coopersmith (1950)

Traditional melody
Arranged by Nylea L. Butler-Moore

and _ on earth, _ in heav - en _____ and _ on earth.

oo - vah ah rets _____ sheh - bah _ shah - mah _ yim oo - vah ah rets.

2. Who knows two? Two I know!
    Two are the Tables of Covenant; One is our God in heaven and on earth.

Sing each of the following lines to the music of the fifth measure. Repeat this measure as many times as necessary for the repeated lines.

Three are the Fathers	Seven are the days of the week	Eleven are the stars
Four are the Mothers	Eight are the days of the Covenant	Twelve are the tribes
Five are the Books of Moses	Nine are the months of birth	Thirteen are the Attributes
Six are the Orders of the Mishnah	Ten are the Commandments	of God

ISRAEL

Vine and Fig Tree

This little round about peace originated in Israel and is known by people around the world. It is usually accompanied by a dance. Sing in unison first.

Hebrew words from Micah 4:3   Traditional melody
English words by Fran Minkoff and Leah Jaffa

And ev - 'ry one 'neath the vine and fig tree, Shall live in

Lo yis - sa goi el _____ goi che - rev, _____ Lo - yil - me

peace and un - a - fraid. (And ev - 'ry) And in - to plow - shares

du od mil - cha - mah. (Lo yis - sa) Lo yis - sa goi el

turn all swords, Na - tions shall learn war no _ more.

goi che - rev, Lo yil - me - du od mil - cha - mah.

 Africa South of the Sahara

Africa is a huge continent, more than three times the size of the United States, with 53 countries and 795 million people. The Sahara, a desert region with few people, tends to divide the continent into two areas—north and south—that are racially, geographically, and culturally different. Sub-Saharan Africa is the home of different peoples of different backgrounds and lifestyles, ranging from tribal peoples, two thirds of whom live in rural villages like their ancestors, to peoples of European descent, who tend to live in large cities.

According to Fred Warren and Lee Warren in *The Music of Africa* (1970), the common denominator for all the tribal inhabitants of sub-Saharan Africa is their love of music and almost total involvement in it. For them "music is not a luxury, but part of the process of living itself." Music follows the African through the entire day, from early in the morning till late at night, and through all the changes of a lifetime, from the moment a baby comes into this world until after the adult has left it.

The sub-Saharan Africans take an active part in making music and reacting to it. Music making is not just reserved for professionals; everyone feels able to write or sing a song. Village children learn by imitating the grownups. They listen to their elders singing and then sing the same songs themselves. There are songs that teach them to count and songs that teach them the history of their people. There are songs that celebrate the birth of a new baby and special songs for a child who loses a first tooth. Little children learn how to play drums or xylophones as they sit in the lap of an adult, who helps them tap out the rhythm by holding their hands or arms.

Every instrument known to the world is found in some form in Africa: horns and guitars, flutes and xylophones, rattles and gongs, and every conceivable form of drum. The thumb piano (*mbira*) was invented by Africans, and its soft and gentle tones have become associated with the "African sound."

The Warrens note that "the most widely used instrument in Africa is the drum. Africans drum when they are happy and they drum when they are sad. . . . An African child will drum on almost anything he can get his hands and fingers on. He will drum on tables, chairs, boxes, packing cases, and kerosene tins. To say that Africans are fond of drumming is an understatement. It's more accurate to say the only time . . . [they don't] drum is when . . . [they are sleeping]!" (p. 51). African rhythms are complicated and difficult for a Westerner to learn; more often than not, the drum and the voice are not following the same beat.

Since the meaning of many African words changes when the voice rises or falls, tunes of chants and songs are often based on these differences in tones. The Ashanti people made use of this characteristic of speech and of varied rhythms to send messages for long distances using their famous "talking drums." According to the Warrens, "however African music is made, by any of the enormous variety of plucked, beaten, strummed or shaken instruments, and wherever it it made, village or city, home or cabaret, it is a vital expression of an indomitable people" (p. 65).

Africans of European descent have their own music, brought by their ancestors from Europe who colonized Africa or conveyed electronically from Western centers. It follows Western styles and is usually a less important part of their lives.

Chay-Chay Koolay

In this singing game of Follow the Leader, the players form a circle with the leader in the center. The leader places hands on head and sings Chay-chay-koo-lay. The other players imitate the action and repeat the words. Then the leader puts hands on shoulders and sings the next phrase. The others follow and repeat the words. On the third phrase the leader puts hands on waist; on the fourth he or she puts hands on hips. Each time the others follow and repeat the words. On the last phrase the leader sits on the ground or floor and everyone else does too. Everyone sits *very* still. Then, without warning, the leader stands up and tries to tag one of the other players, who scamble to their feet and run away. They must *not* start getting up until the leader does. Whoever is tagged becomes the next leader. The words are mainly nonsense syllables.

Traditional words   Traditional melody

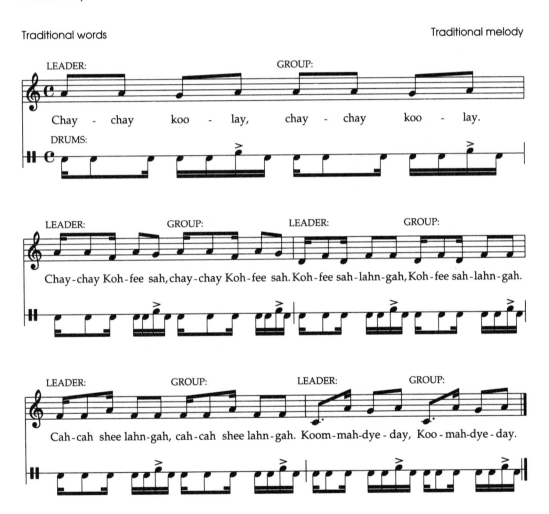

In *Hi, Neighbor*, Book 2 (U. S. Committee for UNICEF).

Sansa Kroma

The words of this Akan song mean, "*Sansa,* the hawk. You are an orphan, and so you snatch up chicks." In nature an orphaned animal must fend for itself. An orphaned young hawk must wander across the sky looking for little chicks to carry off to eat. Akan children singing this song are reminded that if they were orphaned they would not have to wander alone but would be taken in by a relative or another family in the village. For a game called Hawk and Chickens see *A World of Children's Games.*

Traditional words   Traditional folk song

Arrangement © 1986 by Abraham Kobina Adzenyah from *Let Your Voice Be Heard!* Courtesy World Music Press. Used by permission.

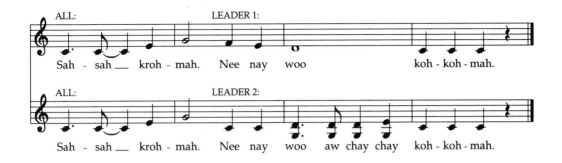

Kra, Kra, Kra, Kra

This is the type of brief call-and-response song that is used at key points in the telling of a story. Such songs are common in storytelling in many parts of Africa. They are often used in stories about Anansi, the trickster character in Ghanian folk tales. (See "How Anansi Spread Wisdom" in *A World of Children's Stories*.) *Kra* does not exactly mean "climb" but is meant to imitate the sound of Anansi climbing a tree. *Tahinta*, which is untranslatable, should have an equally strong rhythmic beat on each syllable. The song could be adapted for other Anansi stories by substituting the appropriate onomatopoeic words for actions.

Traditional words   Traditional melody

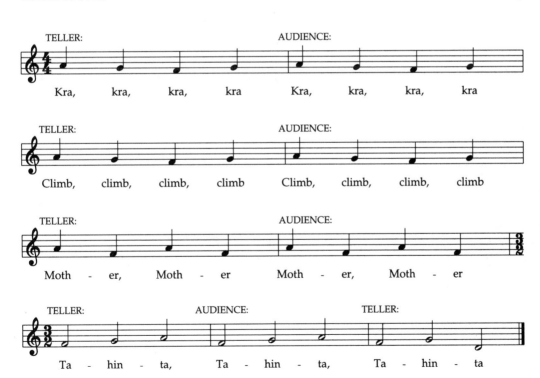

Adapted from a traditional song used by Efua Sutherland in her Children's Theatre Workshop.

Everybody Loves Saturday Night
Bobo Waro Ferro Satodeh

When Nigeria was a British colony, the British imposed an early evening curfew, when everyone had to be off the streets. The Nigerians protested and got the curfew lifted, at least on Saturday, the most important night of the week. This song was written to celebrate their victory and on-going defiance of the British. It has since been carried all over the world and sung in many languages. It is fun to sing in leader - chorus style.

Traditional words

Traditional folk melody
Arranged by Nylea L. Butler-Moore

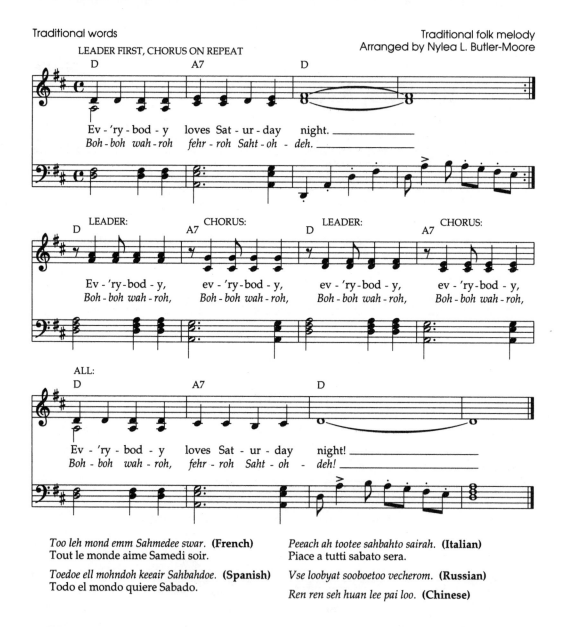

Ev - 'ry - bod - y loves Sat - ur - day night.
Boh - boh wah - roh fehr - roh Saht - oh - deh.

Ev - 'ry - bod - y, ev - 'ry - bod - y, ev - 'ry - bod - y, ev - 'ry - bod - y,
Boh - boh wah - roh, Boh - boh wah - roh, Boh - boh wah - roh, Boh - boh wah - roh,

Ev - 'ry - bod - y loves Sat - ur - day night!
Boh - boh wah - roh, fehr - roh Saht - oh - deh!

Too leh mond emm Sahmedee swar. **(French)**
Tout le monde aime Samedi soir.

Peeach ah tootee sahbahto sairah. **(Italian)**
Piace a tutti sabato sera.

Toedoe ell mohndoh keeair Sahbahdoe. **(Spanish)**
Todo el mondo quiere Sabado.

Vse loobyat sooboetoo vecherom. **(Russian)**

Ren ren seh huan lee pai loo. **(Chinese)**

African Noel

Freed black slaves from the United States settled in Liberia in 1822. Today about 10 percent of the population is Christian. The harmonies and rhythm of this simple Christmas carol are similar to those of an American spiritual.

Traditional words

Traditional folk melody
Arranged by Allen Tuten

Before Dinner

This song from the Lunda tribe of Zaire (formerly the Belgian Congo) describes the traditional duties of women and girls in preparing a meal. One girl states the task and all the others join in the chorus: "Ya, ya, ya, ya."

English words by Carol Hart Sayre

Traditional melody
Arranged by Carol Hart Sayre

First we go to hoe our gar-den, Ya, ya, ya, ya.

Next we car-ry jugs of wa-ter, Ya, ya, ya, ya.

Then we pound the yel-low corn, Ya, ya, ya, ya.

Then we stir our pots of mush, Ya, ya, ya, ya.

Now we eat—come, gath-er round the camp-fire, Ya, ya, ya, ya.

Congo Lullaby

Whatever continent one visits one finds mothers singing their babies to sleep. This simple lullaby is from the Luba tribe. *Mwana* means "baby," *tata* means "father," *bata* means "duck."

Traditional words
English words by Carol Hart Sayre

Traditional folk melody
Arranged by Carol Hart Sayre

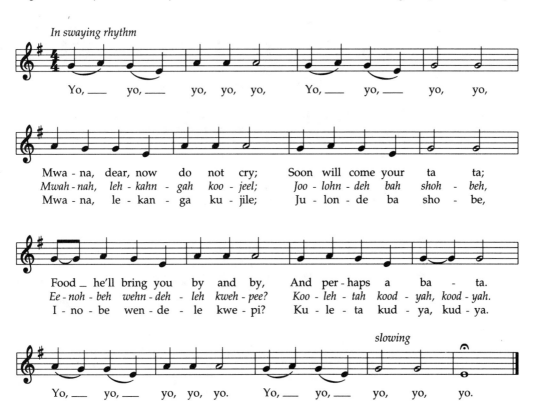

In swaying rhythm

Yo, ___ yo, ___ yo, yo, yo, Yo, ___ yo, ___ yo, yo,

Mwa - na, dear, now do not cry; Soon will come your ta - ta;
Mwah - nah, leh - kahn - gah koo - jeel; Joo - lohn - deh bah shoh - beh,
Mwa - na, le - kan - ga ku - jile; Ju - lon - de ba sho - be,

Food _ he'll bring you by and by, And per - haps a ba - ta.
Ee - noh - beh wehn - deh - leh kweh - pee? Koo - leh - tah kood - yah, kood - yah.
I - no - be wen - de - le kwe - pi? Ku - le - ta kud - ya, kud - ya.

slowing

Yo, ___ yo, ___ yo, yo, yo. Yo, ___ yo, ___ yo, yo, yo.

A Kapasule

In one of the many tribal languages of Angola, *A Kapasule* means "friend" and *moi-o* means "how are you?" Some people believe that the more you sing "A Kapasule," the more your friendship will grow.

Traditional words

Traditional folk melody
Arranged by Nylea L. Butler-Moore

Ah Kah - pah - soo - leh, Ah Kah - pah - soo - leh, Ah Kah - pah - soo - leh, La
A Ka - pa - su - le, A Ka - pa - su - le, A Ka - pa - su - le, La

la la la la la la. Moy - oh, Moy - oh,
la la la la la la. Moi - o, Moi - o,

Moy - oh, Moy - oh, Moy - oh, Moy - oh, La la la la la la la.
Moi - o, Moi - o, Moi - o, Moi - o, La la la la la la la.

Tanzanian Counting Song

Tanzanian children sometimes put small stones on their school desks and count them as they sing the numbers to the tune of this song.

Traditional Swahili words
English version by Mary Lu Walker

Traditional folk melody
Arranged by Allen Tuten

One and two and three and four and five and
Moh - jah, Mbihl - ee, Tah - too, En - neh, Tah - noh

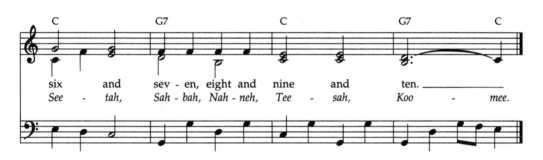

six and sev - en, eight and nine and ten._____
See - tah, Sah - bah, Nah - neh, Tee - sah, Koo - mee.

English version © 1993 by Mary Lu Walker.

Mr. Bamboo Bug
Wavvuuvuumira

In Buganda, that part of Uganda where the Baganda people live, there is a large reddish brown bug that likes bamboo. The name of the bug, *vvuuvuumira*, spoken with lots of "v," suggests the sound that it makes. This song was taught to W. Moses Serwadda by his grandmother when he was a boy in Uganda.

Luganda words as taught to W. Moses Serwadda
English words by W. Moses Serwadda

Folk melody as taught to W. Moses Serwadda
Arranged by Marguerite Clayton

In W. Moses Serwadda, *Songs and Stories from Uganda* (World Music Press, Danbury, CT, 1987 edition). Used by permission.

-65-

At the Market

The market is one of the most important places in any African village or city. The words of this song describe things sold in a traditional outdoor market in a South African village — spices, palm leaf fans, clay bowls, gold rings.

Traditional words
English words by Loise Kessler

Traditional folk melody
Arranged by Nylea L. Butler-Moore

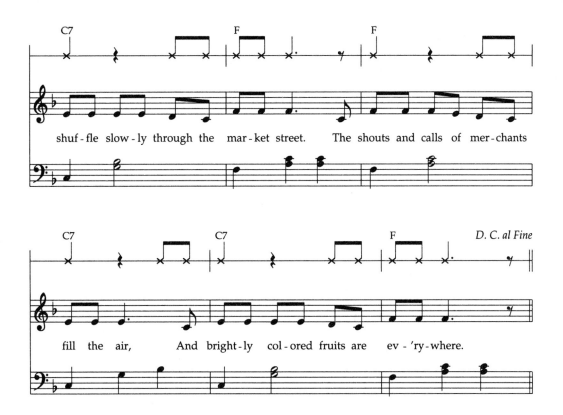

shuf-fle slow-ly through the mar-ket street. The shouts and calls of mer-chants

fill the air, And bright-ly col-ored fruits are ev-'ry-where.

2. "Come, buy my wares!" ("Buy my wares!")
   "Treasures of gold!" ("Buy my wares!")
   "Fruits of the trees!" ("Buy my wares!")
   "Rings of fine gold!" ("Buy my wares!")
   The bargaining and buying never stops,
   The crowds of people throng the outdoor shops,
   The dusty palm trees lend a welcome shade,
   As through long hours the merchants ply their trade.

There Comes *Alabama*
Daar Kom die *Alabama*

Long ago the Dutch settlers in South Africa relied on sailing ships to bring them news, goods, and sometimes a bride. *Alabama* was the name of an American ship that came to Cape Town. The original words are in Afrikaans, which is still spoken by the descendants of the Dutch.

Traditional Afrikaans words

Traditional melody
Arranged by Allen Tuten

There	comes	A - la - ba - ma,	A - la - ba - ma comes
Dahr	*kuhm*	*Ah - lee - bah - mah,*	*Ah - lee - bah - mah dee*
Daar	kom	A - la - ba - ma,	A - la - ba - ma die

o - ver the sea. _____ There comes A - la - ba -
kuhm ohr dee see. _____ Dahr kuhm Ah-lee-bah -
kom oor die sea. _____ Daar koom A - la - ba -

ma, A - la - ba - ma comes o - ver the sea. _____
mah, Ah - lee - bah - mah dee kuhm ohr dee see. _____
ma, A - la - ba - ma die kom oor die see. _____

Sweet, sweet, the sweet-est girl is com-ing back to me, The sweet-est girl in
Nooee, Nooee, dee reet-koee noee dee reet-koee iss huh-mahk, Dee reet koee is furr
Nooi, nooi, die riet-kooi nooi, die riet-kooi is ge-maak, Die riet-kooi is vir

-68-

We Are Marching
Siyahamba

This Zulu song is one of many freedom songs that have expressed black South Africans' hope for freedom from the oppressive white government and a better life. Such songs have been sung by people in prison, by adults and children protesting harsh government decrees, by church choirs, and by people at political rallies. Almost always the singers move with the music, a little rocking motion or small steps from side to side, or more complicated steps. No two groups sing the same song the same way. What the singers feel is more important than how they sing.

Zulu words
English translation by Anders Nyberg

Modern folk melody

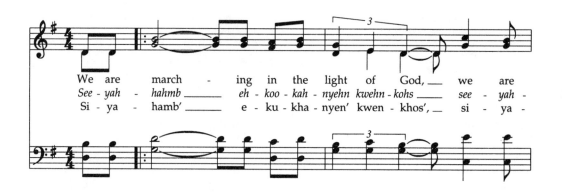

From Anders Nyberg, *Freedom Is Coming: Songs of Protest and Praise from South Africa* (Church of Sweden Mission, n.d.).

Prayer for Africa
Nkosi, Sikelel'i Afrika

The words of this hymn were first written in Zulu in 1897 in the area around Johannesburg then under the Afrikaners' control. It was sung in day schools for blacks and widely popularized by Ohlange Zulu choir. When the African National Congress was formed in South Africa in the early 20th century to protest the oppressive policies of the Afrikaners against the blacks, it adopted this hymn as the closing anthem for its meetings. Today this powerful song is the unofficial national anthem for many African countries south of the Sahara.

Original Zulu words by Enoch Sontonga
English words by Katherine F. Rohrbough

Melody by Enoch Sontonga
Arranged by Nylea L. Butler-Moore

*"Ones" has been substituted for the original "sons."

Swahili words from Ngethe Njroje

Bwana ibariki Afrika
Ili i pate kuamka.
Maombiye tu ya sikelel.
Utubariki, Utubariki.
Ujeh Roho, (Ujeh, Ujeh)
Ujeh Roho. Ujeh Roho, Utujaze.

urope

Each of the 50 countries of Europe has its own heritage of folk music, which has influenced classical music and is still part of Europe's modern urban culture. The themes of European folk songs are similar to those of rural people anywhere in the world—farming and fishing, nature and the seasons, family life, festivals, religion, soldiering, and love. Since earliest times Europeans sang and danced from dusk to dawn at midsummer to celebrate the summer solstice, a custom that lingered on especially in eastern Europe, which was slower to industrialize than western Europe. Later, after they became Christian, Europeans sang and danced to celebrate the birth of Christ about the time of the winter solstice. In Catholic countries high-spirited songs and dances helped mark carnival, a joyful period just before the beginning of Lent.

The specific expression of these common themes reflects the different geography, language, history, and cultural traditions of each country. In addition, at one time or another, the music of every country has been influenced by that of another country because of trade or conquest or sharing a common boundary.

For example, it is not unusual for children who live in the Netherlands, a small country with extensive trade, to speak five languages; often they learn to sing nursery songs in the English, French, Flemish, and German languages of their neighbors, as well as in Dutch. The Dutch have always valued children's songs, and each year they hold a national festival of music composed and performed by children.

The "deep song" *(cante jondo)* characteristic of Andalusia in southern Spain was created by the Moors, an Islamic people whose ancestors came to Spain from North Africa centuries ago. Some songs from the Balkan countries, once occupied by Turks, have Turkish words, and Balkan line dances *(kolos)* traditionally for men are similar to those of the Middle East.

During the 40 years after World War II that the countries of eastern Europe lived behind the iron curtain, their Communist governments subsidized music and other arts but discouraged new forms of artistic expression. The government of the 15 Slavic and Asiatic countries that made up the former Soviet Union encouraged the strong local traditions of song and dance and costume in each country and often in each village, although it did not permit any expression of political independence. Songs written in those years often had patriotic themes, urging people to work together for the whole Soviet Union. Because these peoples had suffered so greatly in World War II and feared another war, songs of peace were popular. The subject peoples were restive, however, under the harsh rule of the central government, dominated by Russians, and in the 1970s the American civil rights anthem "We Shall Overcome" became well known in Soviet schools. In the 1980s when *glasnost* ("openness") became the official policy in the Communist countries, the doors were thrown open to the West. Today pop, rock, jazz, and even rap, imported from the United States, are found everywhere in eastern as well as western Europe.

Today new songs are being written throughout Europe. They will no longer be found chiefly in their country of origin but will be spread to cities and villages throughout the continent by radio and television, a speeded-up, electronic variation of the slower-moving oral tradition. Europeans will be able to communicate through music in a way never possible before.

Shiny Little Moon

Two hundred years ago, when Greece was ruled by Turks, Greek children were not allowed to attend school. They had to go secretly by night. This Greek folk song was sung by children walking to school by moonlight.

Traditional Greek words
English words by Helen Vyronis Halley

Traditional folk melody
Arranged by Allen Tuten

Shi - ny lit - tle moon, to - night In the dark, Oh, lend your light,
Fen - gah - rah - kee moo, lahm - broh Fen - gah moo nah per - pah - toh,

Help us chil - dren find the way ___ Lead - ing to our school, we pray!
Nah pee - gay - noh stoh skoh - lee - oh Nah mah - the - noh grahm - mah - tah!

As we learn or les - sons there God's best gifts may we all share.
Grahm - mah - tah spoo - das - mah - tah Tou Theh - oo tah prahg - mah - tah.

Collected by Charles Hoffman.

Rally Song

This stirring round is based on a "getting together song." The Turkish words mean "my sweetheart to my heart." In the Balkans the leader first sings alone and continues to sing in a high register while the rest of the group, as they assemble, chant the lower notes. This gives an exciting effect, but the song is easier to sing as a four-part round. Sing the round in unison until the melody is learned. Then form four groups with a strong leader to steer each one. Group 1 sings the first line alone and continues, singing the whole round three times. Groups 2, 3, and 4 begin to sing the first line at the places marked in the music and also sing the whole round three times.

Traditional Turkish words   Traditional folk melody

Mee hah - bee   loo - loo beh - shem - bel.   Mee hah - bee loo - loo beh - shem - bel.

Mee hah - bee   loo - loo beh - shem - bel.   Mee hah - bee   loo - loo beh - shem - bel.

From *The Ditty Bag* by Janet E. Tobitt (privately printed, 1945). Reprinted by permission of the Girl Scouts of the United States of America.

I Planted Watermelons
Ja Posejah Lubenice

The music for this song goes with a popular Balkan dance called the kolo. It is danced in a line or circle holding hands, following the steps of the leader. The dancers can be accompanied by a string orchestra, a bagpiper, or a drummer. In some areas, the dancers clap their hands or stomp their feet for accompaniment.

There are many kinds of kolos. Here is one that Serbian children like: Dancers form a circle and sing. On line 1 of the song they take four steps to the right. On line 2 they take four steps to the left. On the word *hay (sehnoh)* they step right, on *straw (slahmah)* they step left. On *oats (zob)* they stand in place and clap hands to the music.

Traditional Serbian words
English version by Mary Lu Walker

Traditional folk melody

Wa - ter - mel - ons ____ soon will be grow - ing,
Yah poh - seh - hah ____ loo - ben - nee - tzeh

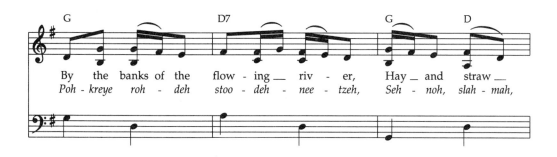

By the banks of the flow - ing __ riv - er, Hay __ and straw __
Poh - kreye roh - deh stoo - deh - nee - tzeh, Seh - noh, slah - mah,

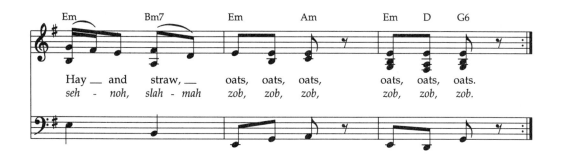

Hay __ and straw, __ oats, oats, oats, oats, oats, oats.
seh - noh, slah - mah zob, zob, zob, zob, zob, zob.

In *Hi, Neighbor*, Book 6 (U.S. Committee for UNICEF). English words adapted by Mary Lu Walker.

Kalina Tree

Ukranians love the *kalina* ("berry") tree for its bright red berries, which cover the branches in summer, hanging in sprays like tiny parasols. People pick the sprays, bind several together, and hang them upside down in their houses to dry. They eat the berries later in the winter.

Traditional Ukranian words
English version by Mary Lu Walker

Traditional folk melody
Arranged by Allen Tuten

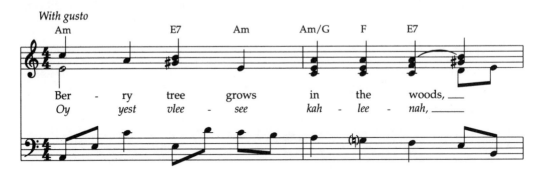

Ber - ry tree grows in the woods, ___
Oy yest vlee - see kah - lee - nah, _____

Ber - ry tree grows in the woods, Ber - ry tree,
Oy yest vlee - see kah - lee - nah, Kah - lee - nah,

Kah - lee - nah, Kahm-eh - ree - kee, tzoo - bree - kee, Kah - lee - nah.
Kah - lee - nah, Kahm-eh - ree - kee, tzoo - bree - kee, Kah - lee - nah.

2.
Young girl saw the berry tree,
Young girl saw the berry tree,
Young girl, Deev-cheen-ah,
Kahm-eh-reekee, tzoobreekee,
Deev-cheen-ah.

3.
Picked the branches one by one,
Picked the branches one by one,
Picked them, Lah-mah-lah,
Kahm-eh-reekee, tzoobreekee,
Lah-mah-lah.

4.
Tied the bundle round with string,
Tied the bundle round with string,
Tied it, Vyaz-ah-lah,
Kahm-eh-reekee, tzoobreekee,
Vyaz-ah-lah.

Many Years
Mnoguyah Lehtah

This song is sung in many eastern European countries in their own languages to honor people on religious and secular occasions. The pronunciation of a Russian version is given here.

Traditional Russian words

Traditional folk melody

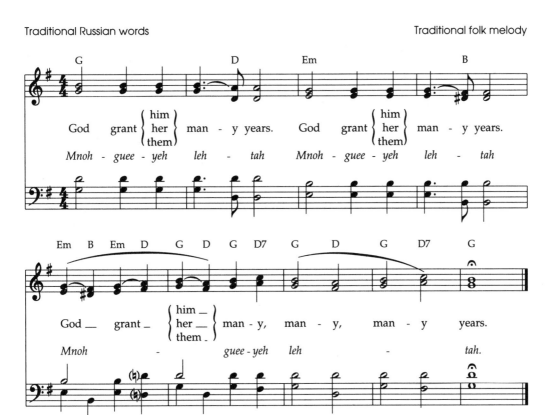

God grant { him / her / them } man - y years. God grant { him / her / them } man - y years.

Mnoh - guee - yeh leh - tah   Mnoh - guee - yeh leh - tah

God __ grant __ { him __ / her __ / them __ } man - y, man - y, man - y years.

Mnoh - guee - yeh leh - tah.

Haying Song

Even today, farmers in some parts of eastern Europe plant and harvest hay by hand as described in this Polish work song. *Tatus* (pronounced "tah-toosh") is an affectionate term for father.

Traditional folk melody

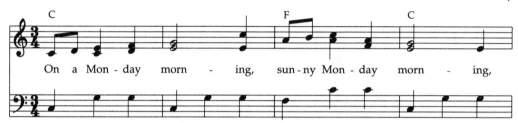

On a Mon - day morn - ing, sun - ny Mon - day morn - ing,

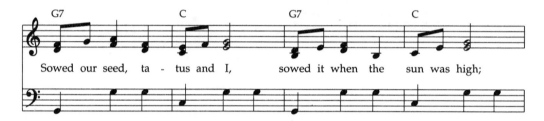

Sowed our seed, ta - tus and I, sowed it when the sun was high;

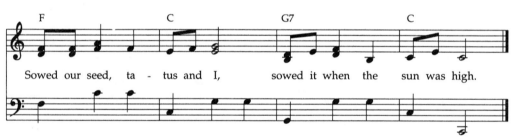

Sowed our seed, ta - tus and I, sowed it when the sun was high.

2. On a Tuesday morning,
   Sunny Tuesday morning,
   Mowed our hay, tatus and I,
   Mowed it when the sun was high. } (2x)

3. On a Wednesday morning,
   Sunny Wednesday morning,
   Dried our hay, tatus and I,
   Dried it when the sun was high. } (2x)

4. On a Thursday morning,
   Sunny Thursday morning,
   Raked our hay, tatus and I,
   Raked it when the sun was high. } (2x)

5. On a Friday morning,
   Sunny Friday morning,
   Hauled our hay, tatus and I,
   Hauled it till the dusk was nigh. } (2x)

6. On a Saturday morning,
   Sunny noon and evening,
   Sold our hay, tatus and I,
   Sold it till the dusk was nigh. } (2x)

7. On a Sunday morning,
   Bright and sunny morning,
   Bowed our heads, tatus and I,
   Thanked the Lord who dwells on high. } (2x)

Farewell to the Old Year
Na Pozegnanie

This is an old favorite everywhere in Poland. It is sung especially on the eve of St. Sylvester, which is the evening of New Year's Day. It is also sung at the closing of the school year.

Traditional Polish words
English version by Mary Lu Walker

Traditional folk melody
Arranged by Allen Tuten

1. How quick-ly time _ is pass - ing. Just like a stream it flows. A
1. Yahk sheeb-koh mee-yah-yoh kvee - leh, Yahk sheeb-koh pwee-nyeh chahs, Zah
1. Jak szyb-ko mi-ja-ja chwi - le, Jak szyb-ko pty-nie czas, Za

year, a day, a mo - ment, Where we'll be no one knows. A
rok zah jayn, zah kvee - leh, Rah - zehm-nyeh ben - jeh nahs. Zah
rok za dzien, za chwi - le, Ra - zem nie be - dzie nas. Za

year, a day, a mo - ment, The fu - ture no - one knows. _____
rok zah jayn, zah kvee - leh, Rah - zehm-nyeh ben - jeh nahs. _____
rok za dzien, za chwi - le, Ra - zem nie be - dzie nas. _____

2. If fortune smiles upon us,
   Someday we'll meet again.
   Once more we'll sing together.
   Remember our song till then.
   Once more we'll sing together.
   Remember our song till then.

English version © 1993 by Mary Lu Walker.

Cuckoo
Kuckuck

This old favorite of Austrian children has been learned by generations of American Girl Scouts. The words of the chorus, except for *kuckuck* (which means "cuckoo"), are attempts to imitate Austrian yodeling. The chorus is accompanied by gestures—slapping knees, clapping hands, and snapping fingers.

English words by Katherine F. Rohrbough

Traditional folk melody
Arranged by Allen Tuten

Oh, I went to Pe-ter's flow-ing spring Where the wa-ter's so good;

And I heard there the Cuck-oo As she called from the wood.

Hoh - lee - ah, hoh - leh - rah - hee - hee - ah, Hoh - leh - rah Koo - koo.

Hoh - leh - rah - hee - hee - ah, Hoh - leh - rah Koo - koo. Hoh - leh - rah - hee - hee - ah,

Hoh - leh - rah Koo - koo,   Hoh - leh - rah - hee - hee - ah   hoh.

2. After Easter come sunny days that will melt all the snow;
   Then I'll marry my maiden fair, We'll be happy I know.
   Holiah . . .

3. When I've married my maiden fair, what then can I desire?
   Oh, a home for her tending and some wood for the fire.
   Holiah . . .

Can You Count the Stars?
Weisst Du, Wieviel Sternlein Stehen?

This much loved song from the 19th century is known by many German-speaking people. Since German pronunciation is difficult, it would be helpful if a German-speaker could teach the children to sing it in German.

German words by Wilhelm Hey
English version by Mary Lu Walker

Traditional folk melody

Do you know how ma-ny stars there are Twink-ling in ___ the mid-night
Vyest doo vee - feel shtehrn - line shtay - en ahn daym blau - en Him - mels
Weisst du, wie - viel Stern - lein ste - hen an dem blau - en Him - mels

sky? Do you know how ma - ny clouds there are? Can you
tselt? Vyest doo vee - feel Vol - ken gay - en vite hin
zelt? Weist du wie - viel Wol - ken ge - hen weit - hin

count ___ as they float by? God is count - ing ev - 'ry
you - bear ahl - leh velt? Gawt, dare hare, ___ hot zee geh -
ü - ber al - le Welt? Gott, der Herr, ___ hat sie ge -

pass - ing cloud Nev - er miss - ing e - ven one. _____ The Cre -
tsay - let, das eem auck __ nicked eye - nes fay - let An - dare
zäh - let, dass ihm auch __ nicht ei - nes feh - let an der

a - tor counts each star, _____ Sil - ver moon . and gol - den sun.
gahn - sen gro - sen tsal, _____ An - dare gahn - sen gro - sen tsal.
gan - zen gro - ssen Zahl, _____ an der gan - zen gro-ssen Zahl.

2. Can you count the butterflies and bees
   Flying in the noonday light?
   Can you count the fishes in the pool
   Where the water's clear and bright?

   God knows every bug and each little fish
   Knows all creatures great and small.
   God who named them knows their number
   Our Creator knows us all.

3. Do you know of other children
   Who live near or far away?
   Do you know if they are happy?
   Do they like to sing and play?

   God loves every child, every girl and boy
   Children here and far away.
   May the God who know and loves them
   Keep them safe by night and day.

O, How Lovely Is the Evening
O, Wie Wohl Ist's Mir am Abend

This is one of the simplest, most appealing rounds there is. It can be sung at Christmas time by changing the second line: "When the Christmas bells are ringing" (Wenn die Weihnachtsglocken läuten).

Traditional German words

Traditional melody

① O, how love - ly is the eve - ning, is the eve - ning,
O, vee vohl ists meer ahm ah ___ bend, meer ahm ah ___ bend,
O, wie wohl ist's mir am A - bend, mir am A - bend,

② When the bells are sweet - ly ring - ing, sweet - ly ring - ing,
Ven zohr roo dee glah - keh loy - det, glah - keh loy - det,
Wenn zur Ruh' die Glock - e läu - tet, Glock - e läu - tet,

③ Ding, dong, ding, dong, ding, dong.
Bim, bahm, bim, bahm, bim, bahm.
Bim, bam, bim, bam, bim, bam.

Rock-a-bye, Baby Bear
Aija, Zuzu, Laca Berni

Mothers and fathers all over the world sing to their babies and promise to bring them good things to eat or drink if they will just go to sleep. The words and tune may be different (see, for example, the "Congo Lullaby" in the African section), but the message is the same.

Traditional Latvian words
English version by Mary Lu Walker

Traditional folk melody
Arranged by Allen Tuten

Lit - tle bear with pad - ded feet, ___ Ay - yah zhoo - zhoo;
Aye - yah, zhoo - zhoo, lah - tcha behr - nee, Aye - yah zhoo - zhoo;
Ai - ja, zu - zu, la - ca ber - ni, Ai - ja zu - zu;

Close your eyes and go to sleep. ___ zhoo - zhoo.
Pah - kye - nah - mee kah - yin - na - mee, zhoo - zhoo.
Pe - kai - na - mi ka - ji - na - mi, zu - zu.

2. Father's gone to look for bees,
   Ay-yah zhoo-zhoo;
   Climbing up the honey tree, Zhoo-zhoo. (2x)

3. Mother gathers berries sweet,
   Ay-yah zhoo-zhoo;
   For her little bear to eat, Zhoo-zhoo. (2x)

4. Baby bear or wolf or dove,
   Ay-yah zhoo-zhoo;
   Little ones need food and love, Zhoo-zhoo. (2x)

Per Fiddler
Per Spelemann

If Norway could be said to have a national musical instrument, it would be the fiddle or violin. This song tells about one man's love for his "good old, fine old violin."

Traditional Norwegian words   Traditional folk melody

1. Per Fid - dler, he once owned a ver - y fine cow. Per
1. *Pair Spell - mahn hahn haht - deh eye eye - nah - steh koo. Pair*
1. Per Spele - mann han had - de ei ei - na - ste ku. Per

Fid - dler, he once owned a ver - y fine cow. He
Spell - mahn hahn hah - deh eye eye - nah - steh koo. Hahn
Spele - mann han had - de ei ei - na - ste ku. Han

trad - ed it in for a used vi - o - lin. He
boot - teh burt koo - ah, feck feh - lah ee - yen, hahn
byt - te burt ku - a, fekk fe - la i - gjen, han

trad - ed it in for a used vi - o - lin. "You
boot - teh burt koo - ah, feck feh - lah ee - yen. Doo
byt - te burt ku - a, fekk fe - la i - gjen. "Du

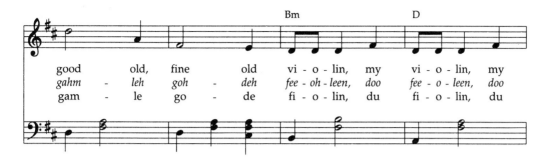

good	old,	fine	old	vi - o - lin,	my	vi - o - lin,	my
gahm - leh	*goh - deh*	*fee - oh - leen,*	*doo*	*fee - o - leen,*	*doo*
gam - le	go - de	fi - o - lin,	du	fi - o - lin,	du

own	vi - o - lin.	You	good	old,	fine	old
*fee - lah	mee.*	*Doo*	*gahm - leh*	*goh - deh*
fe - la	mi.	Du	gam - le	go - de

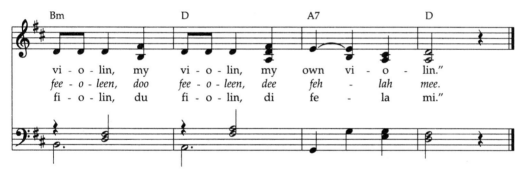

vi - o - lin,	my	vi - o - lin,	my	own	vi - o - lin."
fee - o - leen,	*doo*	*fee - o - leen,*	*dee*	*feh - lah	mee.*
fi - o - lin,	du	fi - o - lin,	di	fe - la	mi."

2. Per played for the dancing. He fiddled all night.
   Per played for the dancing. He fiddled all night.
   Made old folk feel younger, made young hearts grow light.
   Made old folk feel younger, made young hearts grow light.
   "You good old, fine old violin, my violin, my own violin.
   You good old, fine old violin, my violin, my own violin."

3. When dancing was ended old Per took a vow.
   When dancing was ended old Per took a vow.
   And swore he would never trade fiddle for cow.
   And swore he would never trade fiddle for cow.
   "You good old, fine old violin, my violin, my own violin.
   You good old, fine old violin, my violin, my own violin."

Little Short Jacket
Kortjäkje

This Dutch nursery song is sung to an old European tune that Americans and Canadians know as "Twinkle, Twinkle Little Star." *Kortjäkje,* which means "little short jacket," is the nickname of a little girl who, for some mysterious reason, is always sick during the week, but when Sunday comes around she makes a sudden recovery. Could it be that she wants to go to church so that she can carry her beautiful Bible all covered with silverwork? Such Bibles with elaborate silver covers were very popular in the Netherlands.

Traditional Dutch words
English words by Mary Lu Walker

Traditional folk melody
Arranged by Allen Tuten

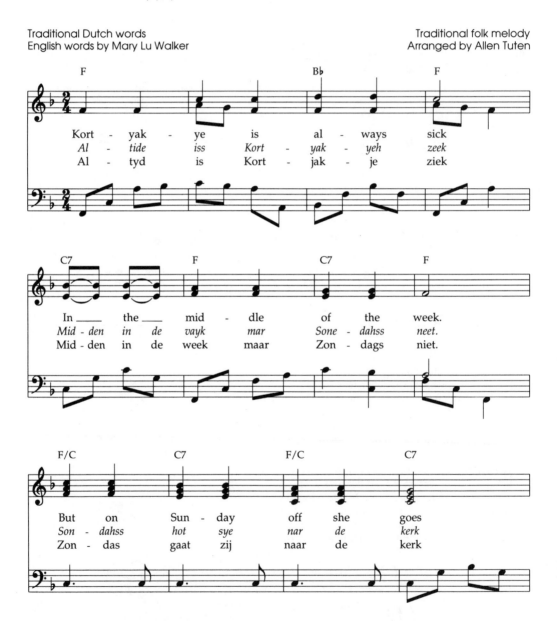

Kort - yak - ye is al - ways sick
Al - tide iss Kort - yak - yeh zeek
Al - tyd is Kort - jak - je ziek

In ___ the ___ mid - dle of the week.
Mid - den in de vayk mar Sone - dahss neet.
Mid - den in de week maar Zon - dags niet.

But on Sun - day off she goes
Son - dahss hot sye nar de kerk
Zon - das gaat zij naar de kerk

English words © 1993 by Mary Lu Walker.

All dressed up in her Sun - day clothes
Met uhn boook fol ___ sil - fer - verk
Met een boek vol ___ zil - ver - werk

But on Sun - day off she goes
Al - tide iss Kort - yahk - yeh - seek
Al - tyd is Kort - jäk - je ziek

All ___ dressed ___ up in her Sun - day clothes.
Mid - den in de vayk mar ___ Sone - dahss neet.
Mid - den in de vayk maar ___ Zon - das niet.

2. She has a little Bible book
   Covered up with silverwork
   And every Sunday off they go
   All dressed up in their Sunday clothes
   And every Sunday off they go
   All dressed up in their Sunday clothes.

O Bambino
One Cold and Blessed Winter

In the 18th century, St. Alphonse, a famous bishop who lived in Naples, wrote the words of a Christmas carol that has been loved by Italians for more than 200 years. He called his song "Tu Scendi dalle Stelle," which means "You Came Down from the Stars." It became popular in America as part of "O Bambino," a carol written in 1964. The words *O Bambino, mio divino, Io ti vedo qui a tremar* mean "O my divine child, I see you trembling."

Words by Tony Velona and Remo Capra

Traditional melody
Arranged by Tony Velona and Remo Capra

1. One cold and bless - ed win - ter _____ in days be - yond _____ re - call, _____ A Child was born to save us, Born _ to save _ us all. _____ One cold and bless - ed win - ter, Born _ to save _ us

2. One cold and blessed winter in ancient Bethlehem,
   A Child was born to love us, Sing, Alleluia, Amen.
   One cold and blessed winter, Sing, Alleluia, Amen.
   O Bambino, mio divino, Io ti vedo qui tremar.
   O Bambino, mio divino, Io ti vedo qui tremar.
   In ancient Bethlehem, a Child was born to love us, Sing, Alleluia, Amen.
   One cold and blessed winter, Sing, Alleluia, Amen.

Dona Nobis Pacem

This round was originally sung in churches in 16th-century Europe. The music is sometimes attributed to G. P. da Palestrina. It is now sung all over the Western world, still in Latin. The words (pronounced *"doh-nah noh-bihs pah-chehm"*) mean "give us peace."

Traditional Latin words   Traditional melody

① Do - na   no - bis   pa - cem,   pa - cem.

Do - na _____ no - bis   pa - cem.

② Do - na   no - bis   pa - cem.

Do - na   no - bis   pa - cem.

③ Do - na   no - bis   pa - cem.

Do - na   no - bis   pa - cem.

The Friendly Beasts

The music for this modern French carol comes from the 12th century and is one of the oldest tunes associated with Christmas. Sunday school children like to dramatize this carol, dressing like the animals and singing like the way they sound. In stanza 6 "beasts" was originally singular.

Words by Robert Davis

Orientus Partibus
Arranged by Allen Tuten

2. "I," said the donkey, shaggy and brown,
   "I carried His mother uphill and down,
   I carried His mother to Bethlehem town;
   I," said the donkey shaggy and brown.

3. "I," said the cow, all white and red,
   "I gave Him my manger for His bed,
   I gave Him my hay to pillow His head,
   I," said the cow all white and red.

4. "I," said the sheep with curly horn,
   "I gave Him my wool for His blanket warm,
   He wore my coat on Christmas morn;
   I," said the sheep with curly horn.

5. "I," said the dove, from the rafters high,
   "I cooed Him to sleep that He should not cry,
   We cooed Him to sleep, my mate and I;
   I," said the dove, from the rafters high.

6. Thus all the beasts by some good spell,
   In the stable dark were glad to tell
   Of the gifts they gave Emmanuel,
   The gifts they gave Emmanuel.

Frère Jacques

This simple little round from France has become one of the best-known children's songs in the world, along with "Twinkle, Twinkle Little Star" (see "Little Short Jacket"). There is a version in almost every language. The Fijian version is about eating food (*tavioka* is a root crop, *bele* is a kind of spinach, *ika*, fish) rather than sleeping boys and bells. Fijian school children also sing an English version, similar to "Brother Peter."

Traditional French words   Traditional folk melody

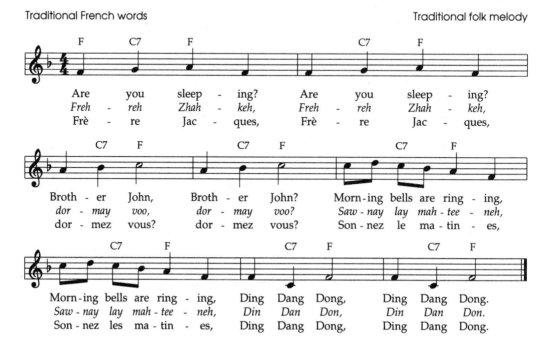

Are   you   sleep   -   ing?   Are   you   sleep   -   ing?
Freh   -   reh   Zhah   -   keh,   Freh   -   reh   Zhah   -   keh,
Frè   -   re   Jac   -   ques,   Frè   -   re   Jac   -   ques,

Broth - er   John,   Broth - er   John?   Morn-ing bells are ring - ing,
dor - may   voo,   dor - may   voo?   Saw - nay lay mah - tee - neh,
dor - mez   vous?   dor - mez   vous?   Son - nez le ma - tin - es,

Morn-ing bells are ring - ing,   Ding   Dang   Dong,   Ding   Dang   Dong.
Saw - nay lay mah - tee - neh,   Din   Dan   Don,   Din   Dan   Don.
Son - nez les ma - tin - es,   Ding   Dang   Dong,   Ding   Dang   Dong.

German

Broo-der, Yah-kob, Broo-der Yah-kob   Bruder Jakob, Bruder Jakob
Shlayfst doo nock? Shlayfst doo nock?   Schläfst du noch? Schläfst du noch?
Horst doo nicked dee glock-en   Hörst du nicht die Glocken
Horst doo nicked dee glock-en   Hörst du nicht die Glocken
Ding Dang Dong, Ding Dang Dong.   Ding Dang Dong, Ding Dang Dong.

Icelandic

May-stah-reh Yah-kob, May-stah-reh Yah-kob   Meistari Jakob, Meistari Jakob
Sah-vairr theeou? Sah-vairr theeou?   Sefur pu? Sefur pu?
Kvahth slarr klug-gan   Hvak slar klukken
Kvahth slarr klug-gan   Hvak slar klukken
Hoon slar threeou! Hoon slar threeou!   Hun staer prju! Hun staer prju!

Spanish

Fray Feh-lee-peh, Fray Feh-lee-peh   Fray Felipe, Fray Felipe
Dwair-mehs too? Dwair-mehs too?   ¿Duermes Tu? ¿Duermes Tu?
Toh-cah lah cahm-pahnah   Toca la campana
Toh-cah lah cahm-pahnah   Toca la campana
Deen Dahn Dohn, Deen Dahn Dohn.   Din Dan Don, Din Dan Don.

Latvian

Brah-lee Yah-nee, Brah-lee Yah-nee
Why too gool? Why too gool?
Ree-ta zvan-nee zvan-nah
Ree-ta zvan-nee zvan-nah
Ding Ding Dong. Ding Ding Dong.

Brali Jani, Brali Jani
Vai tu gul? Vai tu gul?
Rita zvani zvana
Rita zvani zvana
Ding Ding Dong. Ding Ding Dong.

Maori

Hoh-neh eh, Hoh-neh eh
Kay-teh moh-eh koh-eh? Kay-teh moh-eh koh-eh?
Peh-reh tan-gee tan-gee
Peh-reh tan-gee tan-gee
Ding Ding Dong. Ding Ding Dong.

Hone e, Hone e
Kei te moe koe? Kei te moe koe?
Pere tangitangi,
Pere tangitangi
Ave ra, Ave ra.

Fijian

Kah-nah Mahn-dah, Kah-nah Mahn-dah
Tah-vee-oh-kah? Tah-vee-oh-kah?
Kenah-ee-tho-eh nam bell-eh
Kenah-ee-tho-eh nam bell-eh
Nah Eekah, Nah Eeekah.

Kana Mada, Kana Mada
Tavioka? Tavioka?
Kena i ooi na bele
Kena i ooi na bele
Na Ika, Na Ika.

Japanese

Shee zoo kah nah, kah neh no neh
Mah chee no, so rah nee
You meh no yo awn nee
Tahkah coo hee koo koo
Keen kohn kahn. Keen kohn kahn.

Shi zu ka na, Ka ne no na
Ma chi no, so ra ni
Yu me no yo o ni
Taka ku hi ku ku
Kin kon kan. Kin kon kan.

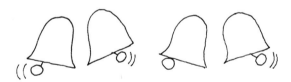

Praise and Thanksgiving
Lobet und Preiset

This three-part round is from Alsace, which over the years has sometimes belonged to France and sometimes to Germany Sing it in unison to learn the melody. Then sing it as a round as an easy way to sing harmony. Each of the three groups begins to sing the first words at the place marked for them in the music and sings the whole song three times through. Try to roll the *r* s.

Traditional German words   Traditional melody

Praise and thanks - giv - ing let ev - 'ry - one bring
Loh - bet unt pry - set, ear Foel - ker dain Hern.
Lo - bet und prei - set, ihr Völ - ker den Herrn!

Un - to our God _____ for ev - 'ry good thing!
Froy - et oich zeye - ner unt dee - net ihm ghern.
Freu - et euch sei - ner und die - net ihm gern.

All to - geth - er joy - ful - ly sing!
Ahl ear Foel - ker, loh - bet dain Hern!
All' ihr Völ - ker, lo - bet den Herrn!

Coulter's Candy

The Scottish dialect may be hard to imitate, but the meaning of the words will make the song easier to sing. "Greetin'" means "crying." "Bawbee" is a small coin. "Tae" is "to." "Mair" is "more." "Puir" is "poor." "Dae" is "do." "Gie" is "give." "Rickle o' banes" is "loose pile of bones." "Sookin'" is "sucking." A "lum hat" is a "stovepipe hat."

Traditional Scots words

Traditional folk melody
Arranged by Allen Tuten

Al - ly bal - ly al - ly bal - ly bee,

Sit - tin' on yer Mam - my's knee, Greet - in' for an -

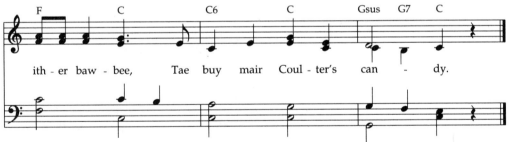

ith - er baw - bee, Tae buy mair Coul - ter's can - dy.

2. Ally bally ally bally bee
   When you grow up you'll go to sea,
   Makin' pennies for your daddy and me,
   Tae buy mair Coulter's candy.

3. Little Annie's greetin' tae,
   Sae whit can puir wee Mammy dae
   But gie them a penny atween them twae
   Tae buy mair Coulter's candy.

4. Poor wee Jeannie's lookin' affa thin,
   A rickle o' banes covered ower wi' skin;
   Noo she's gettin' a double chin
   Wi' sookin' Coulter's candy.

5. Here comes Coulter doon the street
   A big lum hat upon his heid,
   He's been roon' aboot the toon,
   Singin' an' sellin' candy.

The Holly Bears a Berry

There are many versions of this ancient English carol. This one is Cornish. You may know it as "The Holly and the Ivy." The holly is used as a symbol of Christ's birth and death. The word *carol* once meant a circle dance with singing. Such carols formerly accompanied festivals and other joyous occasions throughout the year.

Traditional English words

Traditional melody
Arranged by Allen Tuten

1. Oh the hol - ly bears a ber - ry as white as the milk, And Ma - ry bore Je - sus and wrapped Him in silk; Yes, Ma - ry bore Je - sus, our Sav - ior to be. And the first tree in the green-wood, it was the ho -

ly; Hol - ly; hol - ly; and the

first tree in the green - wood, it was the hol - ly.

2. Oh the holly bears a berry as green as the grass,
   And Mary bore Jesus, who died on the cross;
   Yes Mary bore Jesus, our Savior to be.
   And the first tree in the greenwood it was the holly.
   Holly; holly; and the first tree in the greenwood it was the holly.

3. Oh the holly bears a berry as black as the coal,
   And Mary bore Jesus, who died for us all;
   Yes Mary bore Jesus, our Savior to be.
   And the first tree in the greenwood it was the holly.
   Holly; holly; and the first tree in the greenwood it was the holly.

4. Oh the holly bears a berry, as blood it is red,
   And Mary bore Jesus who died in our stead.
   Yes Mary bore Jesus, our Savior to be.
   And the first tree in the greenwood it was the holly.
   Holly; holly; and the first tree in the greenwood it was the holly.

I'll Tell Me Ma

The children of Belfast, in Northern Ireland, do not live in a peaceful city, torn as it is between Protestants and Catholics, between those who want to remain in the United Kingdom and those who want to join Ireland. In spite of their troubled, often violent world, Belfast children play the games and sing the songs that their families have been playing and singing for generations.

Traditional English words

Traditional melody
Arranged by Allen Tuten

I'll tell me ma when I go home, The boys won't let the girls a - lone. They pull my hair, they stole my comb, And that's all right till I go home. She is hand - some, she is pret - ty, She is the belle of Bel - fast Cit - y. She is a - court - ing

one two three, Please will you tell me, who is she?

2. Albert Mooney says he loves her,
   All the boys are fighting for her.
   They knock at the door and ring at the bell,
   Saying, "Oh, my true love, are you well?"
   Out she comes as white as snow,
   Rings on her fingers, bells on her toes.
   Old Jenny Murphy says she'll die,
   If she doesn't get the fellow with the roving eye.

3. Let the wind and the rain and the hail blow high,
   The snow come shoveling from the sky.
   She's as nice as apple pie,
   And she'll get her own lad by and by.
   When she gets a lad of her own,
   She won't tell her ma when she gets home.
   Let them all come as they will,
   But it's Albert Mooney she loves still.

4. I'll tell me ma when I get home,
   The boys won't leave the girls alone.
   They pull my hair, they stole my comb,
   And that's all right till I get home.
   She is handsome, she is pretty,
   She is the belle of Belfast City.
   She is courting one two three,
   Please will you tell me, who is she?

America North of the Rio Grande

Canada and the United States, which occupy the North American continent north of the Rio Grande, share a common border and many historical and cultural characteristics. Long before the arrival of European explorers and colonists in the 16th century, this vast region was occupied by hundreds of tribes of peoples called Indians and Eskimos by Europeans and now known as Native Americans and Inuit. Each tribe had its own religious beliefs, legends, and music. They believed all melodies belong to the Creator, who sent them to the people, sometimes through the birds, sometimes in personal visions and dreams. Even today tribal songwriters believe they must be in tune with the Creator in order to make songs.

There were hundreds of songs for different occasions, such as planting, harvesting, grinding corn, dancing, or thanksgiving. Many songs were shaped by the land. Songs created by farmers in the dry southwest were quite different from those of hunters in the northern woodlands. Many of the ancient songs of these tribal peoples are still part of their descendants' life, but new songs are being added all the time. Native American music has not been absorbed into the dominant urban culture, but Native American songwriters today often adapt some of the words and rhythms of contemporary American or Canadian music while retaining their own traditional sound.

The tribal peoples were gradually outnumbered, displaced, oppressed, or killed by ever increasing waves of immigrants to the new world. These newcomers brought their various musical traditions with them, each adding another flavor to the musical melting pot. The most powerful ingredients in Canadian music are British and French. The Scots, who settled in Nova Scotia, brought their traditional fiddle tunes for songs and dances that are still found in Canada and Scotland. The French, who settled chiefly in Quebec and New Brunswick, brought their music and language; French is still the official language of Quebec. When some French colonists were driven out by the British in a war, they traveled to Louisiana, where their Cajun music was enriched by that of West African slaves.

In the United States the strongest musical influences were those of the British colonists, seeking freedom and fortune, and those of west African blacks, imported by the colonists as slaves especially to work on the plantations of the South. Scots-Irish small farmers, who settled mainly in the mountains and hills of the South, brought their fiddle music and their ballads, which blended with black music and became the source of present-day country and western music. When some Scots-Irish moved to the southwest, their music mixed with that of Spanish-speaking peoples who had been living there since the region belonged to Spain.

The blacks expressed their African ancestry in the strong rhythms and distinctive harmonies of their music. By changes in rhythm, melody, and harmony they transformed the hymns and Bible stories they learned from their white owners into spirituals. Black music led to the blues, jazz, rock, rap, and gospel music that are such an important part of present-day popular American music.

In the late 19th century more immigrants arrived with their music—Norwegians, Italians, Poles, and other Slavs. After World War II, many displaced Europeans came, among them the Latvians. Known as a "singing people," the Latvians formed singing societies, which carry on their musical tradition. Latin American and Caribbean island people entered in great numbers, bringing calypso, salsa, and other traditional music with them.

Except in Quebec, the descendants of these newcomers did not stay together in ethnic groups. Americans and Canadians love to look for greener pastures. Moving west, far from the nearest neighbor, or to crowded cities for jobs, they have been more concerned with a new life than with national origins. They can learn about their ethnic past through the songs of their ancestors, but they are also partaking of the rich, ever changing brew that is American and Canadian music.

I Walk in Beauty

"Beauty" is an English translation of the Navajo *hohzo*. In the Navajo sense, beauty is more than pleasing physical appearance. It is a state of being in harmony with all living things within the universal circle of life. We might call it being in balance with the environment.

Navajo melody
Transcribed by J. Bryan Burton

Heh   neh - yah - nah,   heh yah   hee   yoh _____   Heh yah nee yoh.

Wakan Tanka Hears Me

Religious ceremonies were important to the Dakota, or Sioux, Indians as a way of communicating with the spiritual world. Ceremonies included songs and dances and might conclude with the giving of gifts such as a painted pipe or buffalo hide robe. The Dakota believed that all gifts came from Wakan Tanka. The translator refers to Wakan Tanka as a male, but the word can be translated as "Great Mystery," "Great Spirit," or "Great Powers."

Words by Paul Glass   Traditional melody

Wa - kan Tan - ka   hears   me,   When I   pray to   him.

Wa - kan Tan - ka   loves   me,   When I'm   ver - y   good.

He   is   strong and   truth - ful,   Bless - ings   he   will   give,

Wa - kan Tan - ka   grants   me   ev - 'ry - thing that's   good.

In Paul Glass, *Songs and Stories of the North American Indians* (Grosset & Dunlap, 1968). © Paul Glass. Used by permission.

Making Maple Sugar

In early spring the Chippewa in what are now Minnesota and Wisconsin set up wigwams under the trees in the forests bordering the lakes. There they tapped the sugar maples for sap to boil down into maple sugar. A Chippewa medicine man sang this chant to help his people obtain a large supply of maple sugar.

English words by Frances Densmore   Traditional melody

1. Let us go __ to the su - gar camp, while the snow _ lies __

on the ground, Live __ in the birch-bark wig - wam

All the chil-dren and the old - er folk While the peo-ple are at work.

2. Make a fire in the sugar lodge,
   So that we may boil the sap.
   Bring all the wooden ladles,
   Set the wooden trough for graining.
   All the people are at work.

3. Cut a notch in the maple tree,
   Set a pail on the ground below,
   Soon the sap will be flowing,
   From the tree it will be flowing
   All the people are at work.

4. In the snow see the rabbit tracks,
   Hear the note of the chickadee,
   We must not stop to follow them,
   'Tis the season of the sugar camp.
   All the people are at work.

5. Bring the sap from the maple trees,
   Pour the sap in the iron pot.
   See how it steams and bubbles.
   May we have a little taste of it?
   All the people are at work.

6. Pour the syrup in the graining trough,
   Stir it slowly as it thicker grows,
   Now it has changed to sugar,
   We may eat it in a birchbark dish.
   There is sugar for us all.

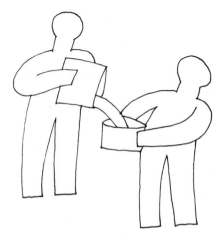

Collected by Frances Densmore, Bureau of American Ethnology, Smithsonian Institution.

She'll Be Coming o'er the Tundra

This is how Inuit children in the northern Alaska village of Koyuk like to sing "She'll be Coming Round the Mountain." *Tundra* is the treeless plain of the arctic regions where the soil never completely thaws. *Muktuck* is whale blubber, an Inuit delicacy, and *agutak* (pronounced *"a-goo'-duck"*) is Eskimo ice cream made from walrus fat and seal oil mixed with sugar, berries, and ice.

Traditional American folk melody
Arranged by Allen Tuten

2. She'll be mushing six white huskies when she comes (2x)
   She'll be mushing six white huskies (2x)
   She'll be mushing six white huskies when she comes.

3. We will have a big fat walrus when she comes (2x)
   We will have a big fat walrus (2x)
   We will have a big fat walrus when she comes.

4. We'll have muktuck and agooduck when she comes (2x)
   We'll have muktuck and agooduck when she comes (2x)
   We'll have muktuck and agooduck when she comes.

Collected by Teri Tibbett.

Canoe Round

Long ago in the pathless forests of what are now eastern Canada and the United States, Indian hunters and French trappers (coureurs de bois) paddled canoes over lakes and rivers in search of game. This song gives a sense of a lone woodsman in his canoe. It can be sung as a four-part round, with each part starting with the first phrase at the point marked in the music for its entrance.

Words by Margaret E. McGee   Music by Margaret E. McGee

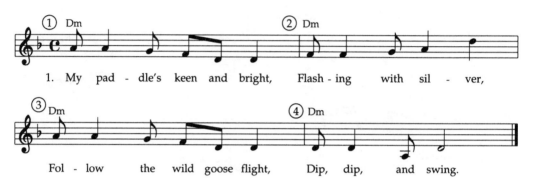

1. My pad - dle's keen and bright, Flash - ing with sil - ver,

Fol - low the wild goose flight, Dip, dip, and swing.

2. Dip, dip, and swing it back,
   Flashing with silver,
   Swift as the wild goose flight,
   Dip, dip, and swing.

Planting Cabbages
Savez-vous Planter les Choux?

This well-known French children's song came to Canada with the French colonists. It is usually done as a simple dance game in which the children act out the words. They join hands in a circle and move to the right singing stanza 1. On stanza 2 they face the center and pretend to dig earth with their fingers and plant cabbages. On stanza 3 they pat the earth with their feet. On stanza 4 they move their elbows up and down. On stanza 5 they nod their heads. Between each stanza they join hands and circle right singing stanza 1. We have given the words in both English and French, but many English-speaking children in Canada and the United States use the French words.

Traditional words

Traditional folk melody

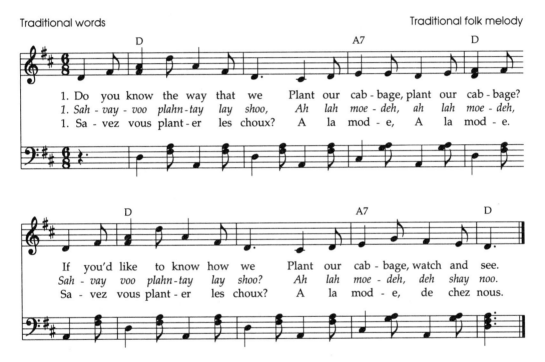

1. Do you know the way that we Plant our cab-bage, plant our cab-bage?
1. *Sah - vay - voo plahn-tay lay shoo, Ah lah moe-deh, ah lah moe-deh,*
1. Sa - vez vous plant-er les choux? A la mod-e, A la mod-e.

If you'd like to know how we Plant our cab-bage, watch and see.
Sah - vay voo plahn-tay lay shoo? Ah lah moe-deh, deh shay noo.
Sa - vez vous plant-er les choux? A la mod-e, de chez nous.

2. We plant cabbages carefully
   With our fingers, with our fingers.
   We plant cabbages carefully
   With our fingers, watch and see.

3. We plant cabbage carefully
   With our two feet, with our two feet
   We plant cabbage carefully
   With our two feet, watch and see.

4. We plant cabbage carefully
   With our elbows, with our elbows.
   We plant cabbage carefully
   With our elbows, watch and see.

5. We plant cabbage carefully
   With our heads, with our heads.
   We plant cabbage carefully
   With our heads, watch and see.

Jack Was Every Inch a Sailor

Most of the people of Newfoundland made their living from the sea. This song, about a sailor on a whaling ship, is one of Newfoundland's many fish stories. Start with the chorus and repeat after each stanza.

Traditional English words

Traditional folk melody
Arranged by Allen Tuten

2. When Jack grew up to be a man
   He went to Labrador.
   He fished at Indian Harbour,
   Where his father fished before.
   On his returning in the fog
   He met a heavy gale.
   Poor Jack was swept into the sea
   And swallowed by a whale. *Chorus*

3. That whale went straight for Baffin Bay
   'Bout ninety miles an hour.
   And every time he'd blow a spray,
   He'd send it in a shower.
   "Oh, now," said Jack unto himself.
   "I must see what he's about."
   So he grabbed that whale all by the tail,
   And turned him inside out! *Chorus*

Study War No More

Many of the spirituals sung by black slaves in the United States were inspired by the Bible. This one was based on the words of the prophet Micah: "They shall beat their swords into plowshares and their spears into pruning hooks: nation shall not lift up a sword against nation, neither shall they learn war any more" (Micah 4:30, KJV). The same words inspired the Israeli song "The Vine and the Fig Tree" printed earlier in this collection.

Traditional words

Traditional folk melody

stu - dy war no more, Ain't goin' stu - dy _____ war no

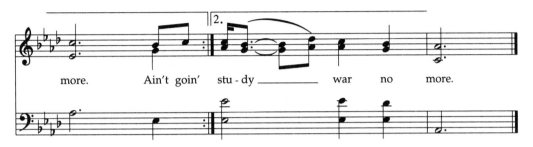

more. Ain't goin' stu - dy _____ war no more.

2. Goin' to put on my long white robe
   Down by the riverside . . .

3. Goin' to talk with the Prince of Peace
   Down by the riverside . . .

Children, Go Where I Send You

This spiritual is a cumulative song similar in form to the Jewish song "Who Knows One?" sung at Passover, printed earlier in this collection.

Traditional words

Traditional melody
Arranged by Marguerite Clayton

With spirit

Chil-dren, go where I send you. How shall I send you?

1. I shall send you one by one, one for the lit-tle bit-ty ba - by,

Ly - ing in a man - ger, wrapped in swad - ling cloth - ing,

and born, born, born in Beth - le - hem.

Repeat as necessary to complete sequence of verses in reverse numerical order.

2. Children, go where I send you.
   How shall I send you?
   I shall send you two by two,
   'Cause two were Paul and Silas,
   One was the little bitty baby,
   Lying in a manger,
   Wrapped in swaddling clothing,
   And born, born, born in Bethlehem.

3. Children, go where I send you.
   How shall I send you?
   I shall send you three by three.
   'Cause three were the Hebrew children,
   Two were Paul and Silas, . . .

4. Children, go where I send you.
   How shall I send you?
   I shall send you four by four
   'Cause four were the four come a-knocking at the door,
   Three were the Hebrew children, . . .

5. Children, go where I send you.
   How shall I send you?
   I shall send you five by five.
   'Cause five were the gospel preachers,
   Four were the four come a-knocking at the door, . . .

6. Children, go where I send you.
   How shall I send you?
   I shall send you six by six,
   'Cause six were the six that couldn't get fixed,
   Five were the gospel preachers, . . .

7. Children, go where I send you.
   How shall I send you?
   I shall send you seven by seven,
   'Cause seven were the seven that went to heaven,
   Six were the six that couldn't be fixed, . . .

8. Children, go where I send you.
   How shall I send you?
   I shall send you eight by eight,
   'Cause eight were the eight that stood at the gate,
   Seven were the seven that went to heaven, . . .

9. Children, go where I send you.
   How shall I send you?
   I shall send you nine by nine,
   'Cause nine were the nine got left behind,
   Eight were the eight that stood at the gate, . . .

10. Children, go where I send you.
    How shall I send you?
    I shall send you ten by ten,
    'Cause ten were the ten commandments.
    Nine were the nine got left behind, . . .

Rise Up, Shepherd

This Christmas carol is a spiritual that follows the call-and-response pattern of many African songs (such as "Chay, Chay Koolay" printed earlier in this collection). It is most effective when a solo voice sings every other line, starting with "There's a star in the east . . . " and the group responds with "Rise up, shepherd and follow" each time.

Traditional words

Traditional folk melody
Arranged by Allen Tuten

fol - low.   Fol - low,   fol - low,

Rise   up,   shep-herd, and   fol-low,   Fol - low the star   of

Beth - e - le - hem, _____   Rise   up,   shep-herd, and   fol-low.

2. If you take good heed to the angel's words,
   Rise up, shepherd, and follow,
   You'll forget your flocks and forget your herds
   Rise up, shepherd, and follow.
   Chorus

Lift Every Voice and Sing

This hymn was written in 1900 by two brothers for a children's choir to sing at a Lincoln's birthday celebration in Jacksonville, Florida. Often called the Negro national anthem, today it is sung and loved by people throughout the country of any age and any color.

Words by James Weldon Johnson

Music by J. Rosamond Johnson
Arranged by Allen Tuten

1. Lift ev-'ry voice and sing, Till earth and heav-en ring, Ring with the har-mo-nies of lib-er-ty. Let our re-joic-ing rise, High as the list-'ning skies, Let it re-sound, loud as the roll-ing sea.

Sing a song full of the faith that the dark past has taught us,

Sing a song, full of the hope that the pres-ent has brought us. Fac-ing the ris-ing sun of our new day be-gun, Let us march on till vic-to-ry is won.

2. Stony the road we trod, bitter the chast'ning rod,
   Felt in the days when hope unborn had died.
   Yet with a steady beat have not our weary feet,
   Come to the place for which our fathers died.
   We have come over a way that with tears has been watered.
   We have come treading our path through the blood of the slaughtered.
   Out of the gloomy past, till now we stand at last,
   Where the bright gleam of our bright star is cast.

3. God of our weary years, God of our silent tears,
   Thou who hast brought us thus far on the way,
   Thou who hast by Thy might, led us into the light,
   Keep us forever in the path, we pray.
   Lest our feet stray from the places, our God, where we met Thee,
   Lest our hearts, drunk with the wine of the world, we forget Thee.
   Shadowed beneath Thy hand, may we forever stand,
   True to our God, true to our native land.

Jingle Bells

This song, written more than 100 years ago, is sung at Christmastime, although the English words make no mention of any Christmas theme. The French version speaks of Father Christmas (the French version of Santa Claus). There are also words in other languages.

English words by James Pierpont

Music by James Pierpont

Jin - gle bells, jin - gle bells, jin - gle all the way.
Tant - ay clohsh, tant - ay clohsh, tant - ay dahn lah nooee.
Tint - ez cloches, tint - ez cloches, tint - ez dans la nuit.

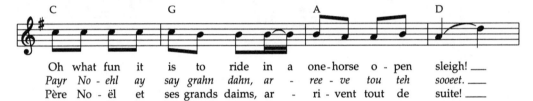

Oh what fun it is to ride in a one-horse o - pen sleigh! ___
Payr No - ehl ay say grahn dahn, ar - ree - ve tou teh sooeet. ___
Père No - ël et ses grands daims, ar - ri - vent tout de suite! ___

Jin - gle bells, jin - gle bells, jin - gle all the way.
Tant - ay clohsh, tant - ay clohsh, tant - ay dahn lah nooee.
Tint - ez cloches, tint - ez cloches, tint - ez dans la nuit.

Oh what fun it is to ride in a one - horse o - pen sleigh!
Payr No - ehl ay say grahn dahn, ar - ree - ve tou teh sooeet.
Père No - ël et ses grands daims, ar - ri - vent tout de suite!

Garden Song

Not everyone has a green thumb, but most everyone who has ever planted a garden hopes that the effort will bear fruit (or vegetable). Sing the chorus first and repeat it after each stanza. The melody is the same for both chorus and stanza.

Words by David Mallet

Music by David Mallet
Arranged by Nylea L. Butler-Moore

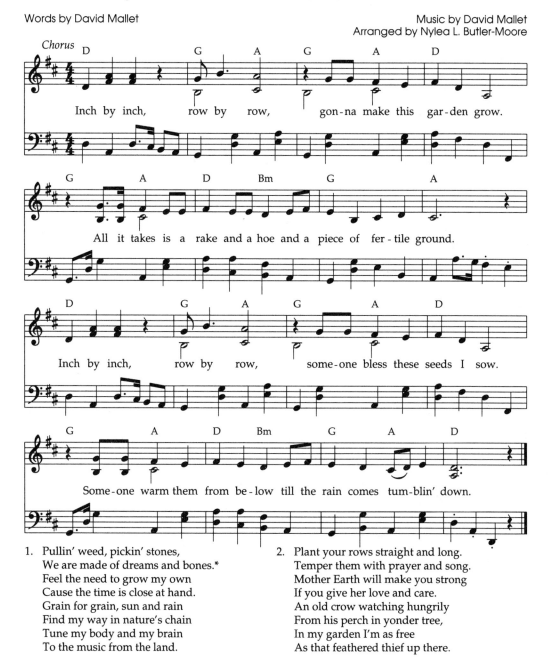

Inch by inch, row by row, gon-na make this gar-den grow.

All it takes is a rake and a hoe and a piece of fer-tile ground.

Inch by inch, row by row, some-one bless these seeds I sow.

Some-one warm them from be-low till the rain comes tum-blin' down.

1. Pullin' weed, pickin' stones,
   We are made of dreams and bones.*
   Feel the need to grow my own
   Cause the time is close at hand.
   Grain for grain, sun and rain
   Find my way in nature's chain
   Tune my body and my brain
   To the music from the land.

   *Original text has "Man is . . ."

2. Plant your rows straight and long.
   Temper them with prayer and song.
   Mother Earth will make you strong
   If you give her love and care.
   An old crow watching hungrily
   From his perch in yonder tree,
   In my garden I'm as free
   As that feathered thief up there.

Magic Penny

That wonderful combination of appealing melody and joyful message makes this song easy to learn and hard to forget.

Words by Malvina Reynolds

Music by Malvina Reynolds
Arranged by Allen Tuten

Love is some-thing if you give it a-way, __ give it a-way, __

give it a-way. __ Love is some-thing if you give it a-way __ You

3rd time to Coda
Fine

end up hav-ing more. 1. It's just like a ma-gic pen-ny,

Hold it tight and you won't have a-ny, Lend it, spend __ it and you'll

have so ma-ny, They'll roll all o - ver the floor. For

CODA

Let's go danc - ing 'til the break of day And

if there's a pi - per we can pay, For love is some - thing if you

give it a - way _ you end up hav - ing more.

2. Money's dandy and we like to use it.
   But love is better if you don't refuse it.
   It's a treasure and you'll never lose it
   Unless you lock up your door.

Share a Little Bit of Your Love

The composer of this song is one of the first people to write liturgical music in the folk manner.
His music is sung in churches of many denominations throughout the world.

Words by Ray Repp

Music by Ray Repp
Arranged by Allen Tuten

Share a lit-tle bit of your love __ my friends, __

Share a lit-tle bit of your love. __ Share a lit-tle bit of your love. __

__ my friends, __ and it -'ll come back to where it be-gan. __

_ 1. And watch _ it grow, _

2. See it shine, see it shine
   See it shine on ev'ry face where it has been.
   Help it shine, help it shine
   Help it shine on ev'rybody, shine on ev'rybody again.

A Place in the Choir

This song, written in 1978, celebrates the animal kingdom. It lends itself to acting out the various animals. Sing the chorus first and repeat after each stanza.

Words by Bill Staines

Music by Bill Staines

Chorus

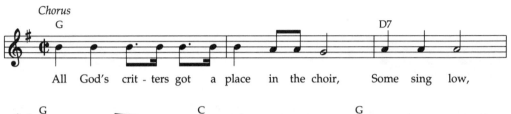

All God's crit-ters got a place in the choir, Some sing low,

Some sing high-er, some sing out loud on the tel-e-phone wire, And

some just clap their hands or paws or an-y-thing they got now.

1. Lis-ten to the bass, it's the one on the bot-tom where the bull-frog croaks, and the

hip-po-pot-a-mus moans and groans with a big to-do, And the

old cow just goes moo. The dogs and the cats, they

take up the mid-dle, while the hon-ey-bee hums and the crick-et fid-dles, The

don - key brays and the po - ny neighs, and the old coy - o - te howls.

2. Listen to the top where the little birds sing
   On the melodies with the high notes ringing.
   The hoot owl hollers over everything
   And the jaybird disagrees.
   Singin' in the night time, singin' in the day
   The little duck quacks, then he's on his way.
   The 'possum ain't got much to say
   And the porcupine talks to himself. *Chorus*

3. It's a simple song of living sung everywhere
   By the ox and the fox and the grizzly bear,
   The grumpy alligator and the hawk above,
   The sly raccoon and the turtle dove. *Chorus*

UNITED STATES

We Give Thanks

Japanese, Spanish, and English are just three of the many languages into which this little grace has been translated. You could try others.

Psalm 75:1   Music by V. Earle Copes

We give thanks to you, O God; _ We give thanks to you, O God. _

Japanese
Kah-mee sah-mah ah-ree gah-toh. (2x)
Ka-mi sa-ma a-ri ga-to.

Spanish
Dah-mohs grah-seeahs ahl Say-nyor. (2x)
Da-mos gra-cias al Señor.

Johnny Appleseed's Grace

The songs from Walt Disney films are part of 20th-century American culture. This grace, short and sweet, is from Disney's *Song of the South,* based on the Uncle Remus stories, written by Joel Chandler Harris between 1881 and 1906.

Words by Kim Gannon and Walter Kent

Music by Kim Gannon and Walter Kent
Arranged by Nylea L. Butler-Moore

The Lord is good to me, and so I thank the Lord for giv - ing me the things I need, the sun and the rain and the ap - ple seed. The Lord is good to me.

A Little Peace Song

This song has been translated into many languages. It may be sung with gestures appropriate to the words, making it easy to understand in any language or even by those who cannot hear.

Words by Mary Lu Walker   Music by Mary Lu Walker

Here is my hand, here is the oth - er. ___

Here is a smile, here is an - oth - er. ___

You are my friend, my sis - ter, my broth - er, ___

May hap - pi - ness and peace be with you.

Reprinted from Dandelions, *words and music by Mary Lu Walker. © 1975 by the Missionary Society of St. Paul the Apostle in the State of New York. Used by permission of Paulist Press.*

America
South of the Rio Grande

The mixing and stirring and blending of many different cultures in America south of the Rio Grande—Indian, European, and African—have resulted in a unique, distinctive music with roots in the distant past and twigs in the electronic present. Hundreds of years before Christopher Columbus "discovered" them in the 15th century, indigenous tribal peoples (later called Indians) were living on the islands of the Caribbean and on the mainlands of North, Central, and South America. Some of them had highly developed civilizations, in which music played an important part. In the Andes Mountains of what is now Peru, the Incas held huge festivals involving thousands of people where drums, flutes, and panpipes accompanied singers and dancers. They made their instruments of shell, bone, clay, and wood. Today their descendants play the same kinds of instruments—vertical flutes, panpipes, drums, and maracas (gourd rattles). A stringed instrument that gives the music from the Andes its distinctive sound is the *charanga* made from a dried armadillo shell. In Mexico, Aztec musicians enjoyed high social status, but they had to be perfect to please the gods. It has been said that if a musician missed a beat of ritual music, he was pulled out of the ensemble and his heart was cut out and sacrificed to the gods.

The mighty cities of the Incas, Aztecs, and other Indian peoples were destroyed by Europeans as they began to colonize the new world. They brought with them different musical traditions from countries speaking Latin-based languages—Spain, Portugal, France—and also from the Netherlands and England. The violins and trumpets played by mariachi bands in Mexico are of European origin, as is the guitar. Before long the Europeans were importing black slaves from west Africa to work in the mines and fields. African music became the strongest influence on Latin American music. Marimbas (primitive xylophones) and leg drums are of African origin.

Depending upon the mix of the population in different countries, wonderful new musical blends came into being. In Cuba, African and Spanish music mixed. In Haiti the influence was French and African; in Jamaica, African and English. The music of Trinidad combines French, Spanish, English, and African traditions. Mexican music mingles traditions of Spanish, African, and indigenous peoples.

Throughout countries colonized by Spain and Portugal and converted to Roman Catholicism by missionary priests, church music has been an important influence. Some of the most beautiful folk songs in these regions are about the birth, life, and death of Christ. Carnival, before Lent, is a joyous celebration. In Trinidad, carnival is celebrated by calypso music, in which the sound of the steel drum blends with the synthesizer and the electric bass as songwriters vie for the prize for creating the best calypso song. Carnival processions in Rio de Janeiro, Brazil, are world famous.

In the grassy *pampas* of Argentina, *gauchos* sing of a cowboy's lonesome life. The meaning of the words may be similar to those of an American Western ballad, but the rhythms are peculiar to Argentina.

Many of the words of old folk songs are sad but have lively tunes. Other songs have haunting, minor-keyed melodies but are written about the beauties of nature—sad tunes to joyful lyrics! Modern songwriters often use such musical contrast to write songs that protest political and economic injustice.

Morning Song
Las Mañanitas

This song is sung in Mexico to celebrate birthdays, often as a morning greeting. It is worth a special effort to learn to sing the Spanish words.

Traditional Spanish words
English words by Janet Tobin

Traditional folk melody
Arranged by Nylea L. Butler-Moore

Alabaré a Mi Señor

This hymn of praise to God is sung in Mexico by people of all ages. "Alabaré a mi Señor" literally means "I will sing praise to my Lord."

Traditional Spanish words
English words by Marguerite Clayton

Traditional melody
Arranged by Marguerite Clayton

English words used by permission of Marguerite Clayton.

and all were — prais - ing God.*
toe-dos ah - lah-bah-bahn al say - nyor.
to-dos a - la-ba-ban al Se - ñor.

Some — were pray-ing,
Oo - nos oh - rah - ban,
U - nos o - ra - ban,

oth-ers were sing-ing and all — were — prais - ing God. _____
oh - tros cahn - tah - bahn ee toe-dos ah - lah-bah-bahn al Say - nyor. _____
o - tros can - ta - ban y to-dos a - la - ba - ban al Se - ñor. _____

*"God" has been substituted for the original "Lord."

The Singing Frog

This is a Mexican version of a story song well known among Spanish-speaking people in the Americas. There are countless other versions. For a South American version that can be used in bilingual storytelling, see "The Singing Frog" in the companion volume to this one, *A World of Children's Stories.*

Traditional Spanish words
English words by Eleanor Hague

Traditional folk melody

When the spi - der goes out for ___ a ___ walk,
Day kay Ah - rah - nyah say sah - lay ah pah - say - ar,
De que A - ra - ña se sa - le a pa - se - ar,

Then comes the frog, and he sings with a
Vyeh - nah lah Rah - nah ee lo say tree -
Vie - ne la Ra - na y lo se tri -

croak. The frog and the ___ spi - der, the frog and the ___
nah. Lah Rah - nah, lah Ah - rah - nyah, Lah Rah - nah, Lah Ah -
na. La Ra - na, La A - ra - ña, La Ra - na, La A -

spi - der, Are sing - ing be - neath the green wa - ter.
rah - nyah, Cahn - tahn - doh day - bah - hoh del ah - gwah.
ra - ña, Can - tan - do de - ba - jo del a - gua.

Chorus   *Repeat ad lib*

Ga - ra, ga - ra, ga - ra, ga - ra, ga - ra, ga - ra.
Gah - rah, gah - rah, gah - rah, gah - rah, gah - rah, gah - rah.

2. When the frog goes out for a walk,
   Then comes the rat and he sings with a squawk,
   The rat and the frog, the spider and the frog,
   Are singing beneath the green water.

Each stanza adds an animal, and the whole list is repeated, followed by the chorus.

3. The rat, the cat
4. The cat, the dog
5. The dog, the stick
6. The stick, the light
7. The light, the water

8. The water, the ox
9. The ox, the pig
10. The pig, the blacksmith
11. The blacksmith, Death
12. Death — God

In Eleanor Hague, *Spanish-American Folk-Songs*, Memoirs of the American Folk-lore Society, No. 10, 1917.

El Tren del Almendral

This little song is about a train running through the fields from the towns of Almendral (stanza 1) and San Josè (stanza 2). Mexican trains say "Chee-kee, chee-kee, chah" instead of "Choo, choo, choo." This song is especially fun to sing in Spanish and to accent with maracas or rattles.

Traditional Spanish words

Traditional folk melody
Arranged by Marguerite Clayton

Pour el ree-el vah corr-ee-en-doe, el trayn dehl
Por el riel va cor-rien-do, El tren del

Ahh-men-drahl, Vah corr-ee-en - doe Vah corr -
Al-men-dral, Va cor-rien - do Va cor -

ee-en - doe cohn Chee-kee chee-kee-chah Chee-kee chee-kee
rien - do con ¡Chi-qui chi-qui-cha! ¡Chi-qui chi-qui

chah Chee-kee, chee-kee, chee-kee, chee-kee, chee-kee, chee-kee, chah!
cha! ¡Chi-qui, chi-qui, chi-qui, chi-qui, chi-qui, chi-qui, cha!

2. Por el riel va corriendo
   El tren de San José (San Ho-say)
   Va corriendo, Va corriendo con,
   ¡Chi-qui, chi-qui, cha!
   ¡Chi-qui, chi-qui, cha!
   ¡Chi-qui, chi-qui, chi-qui, chi-qui, chi-qui, chi-qui, cha!

-143-

Once There Was

This widely known song was introduced to Puerto Rico by French or Italian settlers. It is a good way to learn to count in Spanish.

Traditional Spanish words
English words by Charles Haywood

Traditional folk melody
Arranged by Nylea L. Butler-Moore

In Charles Haywood, *Folk Songs of the World* (John Day Co., 1966).

2. The jolly sailors of this tiny sailboat (3x)
   all decided, decided, all decided to catch fish.
   They caught some big ones, fat ones, long ones, short ones, odd ones of all sizes, (3x)
   and then prepared, and then prepared, and then prepared a tasty dish. (2x)

Casi Lampu'a Lentemué?

This is a question-and-answer song. It goes with the story "Casi Lampu'a Lentemué?" printed in the companion book to this one, *A World of Children's Stories.*

Traditional Spanish and English words
  as sung by Pura Belpré

Traditional folk melody

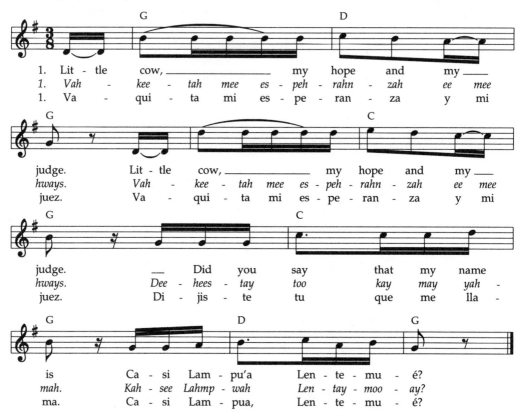

1. Lit - tle   cow, _____   my   hope   and   my ____
1. Vah - kee - tah   mee   es - peh - rahn - zah   ee   mee
1. Va - qui - ta   mi   es - pe - ran - za   y   mi

judge.   Lit - tle   cow, _____   my   hope   and   my ____
hways.   Vah - kee - tah   mee   es - peh - rahn - zah   ee   mee
juez.   Va - qui - ta   mi   es - pe - ran - za   y   mi

judge.   ___   Did   you   say   that   my   name
hways.   Dee - hees - tay   too   kay   may   yah -
juez.   Di - jis - te   tu   que   me   lla -

is   Ca - si   Lam - pu'a   Len - te - mu - é?
mah.   Kah - see   Lahmp - wah   Len - tay - moo - ay?
ma.   Ca - si   Lam - pua,   Len - te - mu - é?

2. I am not your hope or your judge (2x)
   Nor did I say that your name is
   Casi Lampu'a Lentemué. (2x)

3. Little goat, my hope and my judge (2x)
   Did you say that my name is
   Casi Lampu'a Lentemué? (2x)

4. I am not your hope or your judge (2x)
   Nor did I say that your name is
   Casi Lampu'a Lentemué. (2x)

5. Little pig, my hope and my judge (2x)
   Did you say that my name is
   Casi Lampu'a Lentemué? (2x)

6. I am not your hope or your judge (2x)
   Nor did I say that your name is
   Casi Lampu'a Lentemué. (2x)

7. Little crab, my hope and my judge (2x)
   Did you say that my name is
   Casi Lampu'a Lentemué? (2x)

8. Yes, I am your hope and your judge (2x)
   And I did I say that your name is
   Casi Lampu'a Lentemué. (2x)

Collected by Anne Pellowski.

Brown Girl

Sugar and rum are both made in Trinidad, and this lively game song from Port-of-Spain, the capital, gives both products of sugar cane equal time. It is sung to a calypso beat. One child standing in the center of a circle of children makes motions, which the others copy. The chorus is sung at the beginning of the song and after each stanza. "Ling" is heather. You may wish to have the children sing "plums" instead of "rum."

Traditional words

Traditional folk melody
Arranged by Marguerite Clayton

1. Show me a motion, sing and make it fun (3x)
   Oh, she likes sugar and I like rum. *Chorus*

2. Clap and snap your fingers (clap, clap, clap, clap, clap, snap) (3x)
   Oh, she likes sugar and I like rum. *Chorus*

3. Hug and kiss your partner (smack, smack, smack, smack, smack) (3x)
   Oh, she likes sugar and I like rum. *Chorus*

4. Down by the ocean, take a little swim (3x)
   Oh, she likes sugar and I like rum. *Chorus*

5. Say you love your brown girl (pss, pss, pss, pss, pss) (3x)
   Oh, she likes sugar and I like rum. *Chorus*

6. Make another motion, sing and make it fun (3x)
   Oh, she likes sugar and I like rum. *Chorus*

As sung by the Choral Society at the Nausica Teachers' College, Port-of-Spain, and collected by Evelyne and Bob Beers.

Mary Had a Boy-Child

This West Indian Christmas carol is sung to a calypso beat. The song begins with the chorus, which is repeated after each stanza.

Traditional words

Traditional folk melody
Arranged by Allen Tuten

-148-

Last Chorus

Jees - a Chrise, __ He born on Chris - a - mus Day!

Mar - y had a boy - child Jees - a Chrise, __ He's a born on Chris - a - mus Day, (My, my, __ my, my!) Joy to the world! Born on Chris - a - mus Day!

2. While shepherds watched dere flocks by night, them see a bright new shining star,
   Then de herald choir sing, de music seem to come from afar. *Chorus*

3. Now Joseph and he wife Mary, came to Betlehem that night,
   They find no place for to born, to child; not a single room was in sight. *Chorus*

4. By 'n by they find a little nook, in a stable all forlorn,
   And in a manger cold and dark, Mary's little boy-child was born. *Chorus*

5. The tree [*sic*] wise men tell old King Herod, we hear a new King born today,
   We bring he frankensense and myrh, we come from far, far away. *Chorus*

6. When old King Herod him learned this news, him mad as him can be,
   He tell de wise men find this child, so that I may worship he! *Chorus*

7. Long time ago in Betlehem, so de holy Bible say,
   Mary's boy-child Jeesa Chrise, He born on Chrisamus Day. *Last Chorus*

Tinga Layo

Little donkeys loaded down with bundles and people are a common sight along the roads on the islands of the West Indies, as they are in developing countries around the world.

Traditional words

Traditional folk melody
Arranged by Marguerite Clayton

Ting - a lay o, come, lit - tle don - key, come. Ting - a

lay o, come, lit - tle don - key, come. My don - key

walk, my don - key talk, my don - key eat __ with a knife and fork. My don - key

walk, my don - key talk, my don - key eat __ with a knife and fork. Ting - a

lay - o, come, lit - tle don - key, come. Ting - a

lay - o, come, lit - tle don - key, come.

All the Colors
De Colores

This song vividly describes the beauty of the countryside in the spring.

Traditional Spanish words
English version by Mary Lu Walker

Traditional folk melody
Arranged by Allen Tuten

All _____ the col - ors _____ all the col - ors I
Deh _____ coh - lohr - ehs, _____ deh coh - lohr - ehs seh
De _____ co - lor - es, _____ de co - lor - es se

see in the flow - ers and trees in the spring - time. _____
vees - tehn lohs cahm - pohs en lah pree - mah - vair - ah, _____
vis - ten los cam - pos en la pri - ma - ve - ra, _____

All _____ the col - ors _____ all the col - ors of
Deh _____ coh - lohr - ehs _____ deh coh - lohr - ehs sohn
De _____ co - lor - es, _____ deh co - lor - es son

birds fly - ing high in the sky as they sing. _____
lohs pah - hah - ree - yohs kay vyen en deh fway - rah. _____
los pa - ja - ri - llos que vien - en de fue - ra. _____

Hear Aunty Bess

Children in Guyana sing about Aunty Bess, who seems hard to please and doesn't keep her troubles to herself. The words are in Guyanese dialect, which is based on English. "Ah halla" means "holler" or "shout." "'Fo' day" means "before day."

Traditional words modified by
   Marguerite Clayton

Traditional folk melody
Arranged by Marguerite Clayton

Repeat stanza 1.

Sing, Sing, Sing

This *roda,* or circle game, with its counting-out rhyme, provides a musical framework for choosing a soloist to begin a performance of songs and dances. It is comparable to counting-out games to choose It for a children's game elsewhere in the world. It also teaches the names of some South American countries. "Senhoras" means "ladies."

In Beatrice Landeck, *Echoes of Africa* (David McKay and Co., 1961).

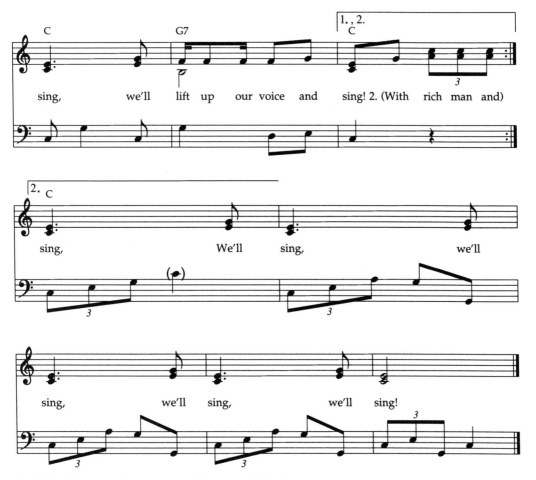

sing,   we'll   lift   up   our   voice   and   sing! 2. (With   rich   man   and)

2. C

sing,   We'll   sing,   we'll

sing,   we'll   sing,   we'll   sing!

2. With rich man and poor man and beggar and thief,
    With doctor and lawyer and merchant and chief,
    We'll sing, we'll sing, we'll lift up our voice and sing!

3. In Uruguay, Paraguay, Chile, Peru,
    Brazil, Venezuela, Bolivia, too,
    We'll sing, we'll sing, we'll lift up our voice and sing!
    We'll sing, we'll sing, we'll sing, we'll sing!

The Butterfly
La Mariposa

This song is about the *morenada,* a dance brought to Peru from West Africa by slaves. It's a trickster song in the tradition of "Simon Says" as the leader tries to mix up the listeners by singing "con los manos" ("with the hands") while the listeners clap and "con los tacos" ("with the heels") while they stamp. The first few times the leader sings as the song is written but then he or she might say "con los tacos" first while the group invariably claps instead of stamps. Everyone joins in on "la la la . . . " and has a great time.

English version by Mary Lu Walker

Traditional folk melody
Arranged by Nylea L. Butler-Moore

La la la la la   la la   la la la la la la la la la.

La la la la la   la la   la la la la la la la la la!

Canta, Canta, Pajarito

This delightfully rhythmic song has a dance to go with it. Children form a line. They step to the right with the right foot, slide the left to close, step on the right, stand still, and clap three times. Then they reverse the pattern, stepping to the left with the left foot, sliding the right to close, stepping on the left, standing still, and clapping three times. They repeat the whole pattern, right and left, four times. Instead of dancing the children could use maracas, sticks, triangles, or clapping to mark the rhythm. "Canta, canta, pajarito" means "sing, sing, little bird."

Words adapted by Isabelle Jerahian LaMont

Traditional folk melody
Arranged by Nylea L. Butler-Moore

Can - ta, can-ta lit-tle bird. Can - ta, can-ta pa-ja-
Cahn - tah, can-tah *Cahn - tah,cahn-tah pah-hah -*

ri - to, Now we know the spring will be here soon.
ree-toh,

My Farm
Mi Chacra

This song about farmyard animals is known in several South American countries and in Mexico. The stanzas all start and end the same way but introduce a different animal. Even if you sing it in English it is fun to use the names of the animals in Spanish.

Traditional Spanish words

Traditional folk melody
Arranged by Allen Tuten

1. Come, come and see my farm, for it is love - ly,
1. *Ven - gahn ah vair mee chah - crah case air - moh - sah*
1. Ven - gan a ver mi cha - cra que_es her - mo - sa

Come, come and see my farm, for it is love - ly.
Ven - gahn ah vair mee chah - crah case air - moh - sah.
Ven - gan a ver mi cha - cra que_es her - mo - sa.

The _____ chick - en goes like __ this: peep - peep!
El pol - yee - toh ah - seh ah - see: peep - peep!
El po - lli - to ha - ce a - si: peep - peep!

The _____ chick - en goes like __ this: peep - peep!
El pol - yee - toh ah - seh ah - see: peep - peep!
El po - lli - to ha - ce a - si: peep - peep!

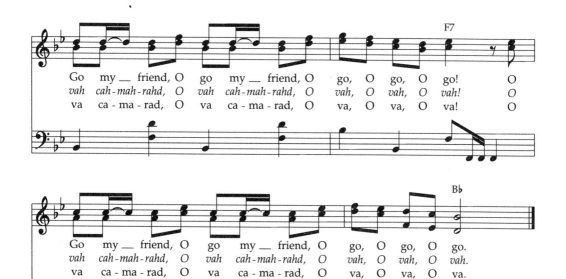

Go	my __ friend, O	go	my __ friend, O	go, O	go, O	go!	O
vah	*cah-mah-rahd,* O	*vah*	*cah-mah-rahd,* O	*vah,* O	*vah,* O	*vah!*	O
va	ca - ma - rad, O	va	ca - ma - rad, O	va, O	va, O	va!	O

Go	my __ friend, O	go	my __ friend, O	go, O	go, O	go.
vah	*cah-mah-rahd,* O	*vah*	*cah-mah-rahd,* O	*vah,* O	*vah,* O	*vah.*
va	ca - ma - rad, O	va	ca - ma - rad, O	va, O	va, O	va.

2. Come, come and see . . .
   El pah-tee-toh (*patito*, "duckling") goes like this: quack, quack!
   O go my friend . . .

3. El oh-see-toh (*osito*, "little bear") goes like this: grr, grr!

4. El cah-bah-yoh (*caballo*, "horse") goes like this: neighhh!

5. Ee el boo-roh (*y el burro*, "and the donkey") goes like this: hee, haw!

6. Leh-chon-see-toh (*lechoncito*, "piglet") goes like this: oink, oink!

7. El gah-tee-toh (*gatito*, "kitten") goes like this: meow!

8. Leh-choo-see-toh (*lechucito*, "owlet") goes like this: hoo-hoo!

9. Ee el toh-roh (*y el toro*, "and the bull") goes like this: ro-ahrrr!

# Oceania

The peoples of Oceania inhabit Australia, New Zealand, the Malay Archipelago, the Philippines, and hundreds of small islands that float like tiny boats in the vast south Pacific ocean. From the 16th century to World War II, these peoples were increasingly under European control. Today, most of them have become independent.

For thousands of years Australia was inhabited only by Aborigines, a nomadic people who lived as hunters, gatherers, and fishers. Music and dance have been an integral part of their life, and even today they use ancient chants to keep their traditions alive and teach their children about modern ways of living. Some groups accompany their chants on the *digeridoo*, a unique instrument made of a hollowed-out gumtree branch, which, when blown into, produces a rhythmic drone. Other groups strike clapsticks together for a strong, regular accompaniment.

The island peoples—Melanesians and Micronesians north of Australia and Polynesians to the east—may have migrated there from Africa and Asia thousands of years ago. Miles of ocean separated the island groups, where people developed related but distinct cultures. They preserved their traditions in chants and dances concerned with love, sadness, wars, and the mighty deeds of their ancestors. New songs are still written to mark special events. The Maoris of New Zealand memorialized the exploits of their fierce warriors and skilled seafarers in dramatic *haka* chants and exciting dances, although Maori music today is noted for lovely melodies and gentle harmonies. Hawaiians perfected graceful hula dances and accompanying songs as part of their religious ceremonial.

Human voices and drums have always been the chief sources of music in Oceania. Traditional instruments were made from materials available in the bush, beach, or jungle. Rotuman women and men beat with sticks on rolled-up, woven grass mats. Drummers in Fiji beat intricate tatoos on a hollowed-out log, the *lali* drum. Drums set the beat for dancers and singers in Samoa. Men and boys in the Solomon Islands blow bamboo panpipes as they walk and sway to their music.

Immigrants from England, Scotland, and Ireland brought their folk songs and music hall songs to Australia and New Zealand. These traditions along with classical Western music have become dominant in these countries. On the other islands, even today, music is as important a part of everyday life as the tides and the tropical sun. Children learn the songs of their people by following their parents in the dance or beating sticks on the ground in time to the music. By the time they are teenagers they can take their place alongside the adults in the dancing and singing that are a major part of any gathering.

Traditional instruments have been augmented or modified by European imports. In Samoa, dances and songs are accompanied by guitars and ukeleles, said to have been brought to the Pacific by Portuguese seamen. Often handmade from the polished hull of a coconut, ukeleles are still one of the most popular island instruments. In Vanuatu virtuoso bottle players play jaunty tunes that reflect French influence. Musicians in the Solomons play a giant bamboo panpipe by thumping the open end of the pipe with the rubber sole of a flip-flop sandal, often to a boogie beat. In many island musical groups the string bass is made from an empty tea chest rigged out with clothesline attached to a sturdy tree branch. All these elements give the music of Oceania its distinctive character.

Lompat Hai Katak

Planting and harvesting rice is hard work and on the island of Sumatra workers spend many hours in the fields. They often sing a song like "Lompat Hai Katak" ("Jump, Little Frog!") to make the time go more quickly. You might like to sit down on the floor and, on the beat, toss a bean bag back and forth to a partner, pretending it's a frog!

Words simplified from the original Indonesian

Traditional folk melody
Arranged by Nylea L. Butler-Moore

Used by permission of Marilyn Shepherd, music specialist, Carlesbad, Calif.

My Nipa Hut
Bahay Kubo

Farming peoples are likely to sing songs about crops; this Tagalog song lists the vegetables growing in gardens in the Philippines. *Singkamas* means "beans"; *talong*, "egg plant"; *sigarillas*, "spinach"; *mani*, "peanuts"; *stiao*, "string beans"; *batao*, "lima beans"; *patani*, "turnips." *Nipa* is thatch made from the East Indian palm. The song, of which there are many versions, is as well known among Filipinos in Hawaii as in their homeland.

Traditional Tagalog words
English words by Aurelia Viernes

Traditional melody
Arranged by Allen Tuten

2. All kinds of good things are found everywhere,
    Of cabbage and squash there is plenty to spare,
    Cucumbers and peas so tender and sweet,
    And everything else good to eat.

"My Nipa Hut" from *Folk Songs Hawaii Sings* by John Kelly. Used by permission of Charles E. Tuttle Co., Inc. of Tokyo, Japan.

Little Heron
Na Belo

"Little Heron" is a children's *meke* (pronounced "meh-keh"), a traditional Fijian story-chant-dance. One of the important parts of the *meke* is the rhythm, which can be tapped out on a *lali,* (pronounced "lah-lee") drum with two sticks or even with two pencils on a desk top. The Fijian words tell the story of a black heron and a white heron. The English is not a direct translation. The sound "click" should resemble clucking to a horse.

Traditional Fijian words
English version by Mary Lu Walker

Traditional melody

1. Lit - tle her - on ____ fly - ing up so high.
1. *Nah bel - oh, nah bel - oh ____ lye - lye.*

Come and perch be - side me, Leave the sun - ny sky. We'll have
Voo - kah voh - lee mye. ____ Vah - kah - moo - ree whye. Lye roh

fun ____ just you ____ and ____ I. You and I
en - nah tahm - bahn - ee teer - ee whye. Lay ____ roh!

(Click, click, click) You and I! (Click, click, click.)
(Click, click, click) Lay! ____ roh! (Click, click, click.)

2. Oh, no, I don't think I will go.
   If I fly too low,
   You may try to catch me,
   And never let me go,
   Oh, no! (Click, click, click)
   Oh, no! (Click, click, click.)

3. There are two little herons in the sky,
   One of them is black
   One of them is white
   Friends forever
   Together day and night
   Never fight! (Click, click, click)
   Never fight! (Click, click, click.)

We Are One Big Happy Family

Children in the Pacific islands sing this song, taught them by missionaries, with broad gestures, pointing at one another, shaking hands, and so on.

Traditional Western hymn melody
Arranged by Allen Tuten

We are one big hap - py fam - i - ly, one big fam - i - ly,

God's fam - i - ly. We are one big hap - py fam - i - ly,

God's fam - i - ly are we. 1. She is my

sis - ter, he is my broth - er, my

2. We are . . .
   She is my sister, you are my brother, my father and mother, . . .

3. We are . . .
   They are my sisters, they are my brothers, our father and mother, . . .

Jesus Loves Everyone
Jesus Like 'Em Allketa

This Sunday school song is known by children throughout the Pacific islands. We have printed the words in Bislama (one of the languages used in Vanuatu) and various other Pacific languages to show you how they look.

Traditional words

Western hymn melody
Arranged by Allen Tuten

you, he loves me. Je - sus likes us all. _____
you, like 'em me, like 'em al - ke - tah. _____

Fijian

Jisu sa lomani keda
Lomani keda, lomani keda
Jisu sa lomani keda
Lomani keda kecekecega.
Lomani Tata
Lomani Nana
Lomani Tuakaqu
Taciqu talega
E lomani iko
E lomani au
Lomani keda kecekecega.

Samoan

Alofa Iesu mo tatou uma
tatou uma tatou uma
Alofa Iesu mo tatou uma
Alofa Iesu mo tatou.
Alofa Ia tama
Alofa Ia Tina
Alofa Lou Uso
Malou Tuagane
Alofa Ia teoe
Alofa Ia teau
Alofa Iesu Mo tatou.

Tongan

Sisu ofa Ia tautolu
Ia tautolu, Ia tautolu
Sisu ofa Ia tautolu
Ofa Ia tautolu kotoa.
Ofa ie tamai
Ofa ie tina
Ofa tokoua
Ofa tuogane
Ofa Ia oe
Ofa Ia au
Ofa Ia tautolu kotoa.

Png

Esu na Euramu Iboudai
Iboudai, Iboudai
Esu na Euramu Iboudai.
Euramu Ibodai
Euramu Tamaqu
Euramu Sinaqu
Euramu Kakaqu
Euramu Tadigu
Euramu oe
Euramu Lau
Euramu Iboudai.

Ting-a-la-la-la

Many people on the islands of the South Pacific earn their living by fishing. This is one of many, many songs about fish and fishing. It tells the story of a fisherman sitting on a dock in the bright morning sunshine. A little dog comes along and nips him and SPLASH, he falls into the warm ocean waters.

English words by Mary Lu Walker

Traditional melody
Arranged by Marguerite Clayton

1. If you go out fish-ing on a bright and sun-ny day,
and see lit-tle fish-es all a-swim-ming 'round the bay,
Hands are in their pock-ets and their pock-ets in their pants,
Lit-tle fish are do-ing you a hap-py is-land dance!

Chorus

Ting - a - ting - a - ting - a - la - la, Ting - a - la - la - la!

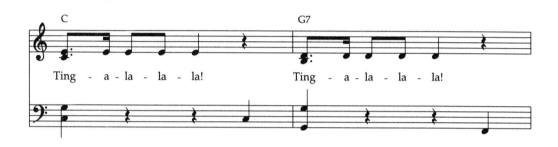

Ting - a - la - la - la! Ting - a - la - la - la!

Ting - a - ting - a - ting - a - la - la, Ting - a - la - la - la,

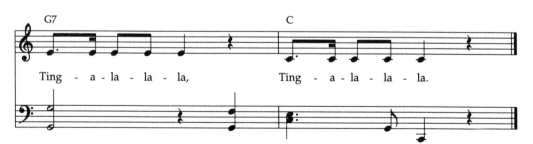

Ting - a - la - la - la, Ting - a - la - la - la.

2. Sitting on a little bridge as happy as can be,
   Throwing out my hook and line to catch a fish for tea,
   'Long came a little dog and took a bite of me,
   Lost my hook and lost my line and fell into the sea. *Chorus*

Pokarekare

Although this is a love song about a boy waiting for his sweetheart, New Zealanders of all ages sing it. Children learn it in school and camp. The world famous New Zealand opera star Kiri Te Kanawa often sings it as a final encore after her concerts. The refrain should be sung twice.

Traditional Maori words
English version by Mary Lu Walker

Music by P. H. Tomana
Arranged by Allen Tuten

1. How qui-et are the wa - ters of rip-pling Wai -
1. Poh - kah-ray-kah-ray ah - nah ngah wye oh Wye -

a - pu, Now's the time of your re - turn - ing,
ah - poo Whee - tee ah - too-koh - ay hee - nay,

I'm wait-ing here for you. Oh, my dear
Mah - ree-noh ah-nah ay. Ay hee - nay

love, Come soon to me
ay, Hoh - kee mye - rah,

Or I will sure - ly die for __ love of thee.
Kah mah - tay ah - oo ee tay ah - roh - hah ay.

2. I'm writing you a letter
   I'm sending you a ring.
   If your mother ever finds it,
   Then troubles will begin.
   Refrain

Canoe Song

The Maori people of New Zealand sang this canoeing song long ago. You might want to compare it to the "Canoe Round" from Canada earlier in this book. Today it is sung by English-speaking New Zealanders as well, often to the accompaniment of the ukelele. The words *i-to-ma-u-na-wa* (pronounced "ee-toh-mah-oo-nah-wah") are sounds without meaning.

Traditional melody

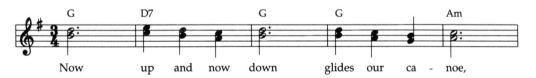

Now up and now down glides our ca - noe,

On - ward to Wai - a - ri - ki; See, see how the waves

part from her prow, Sing __ i - to - ma - u - na - wa

Mumma Warrunno

This is a lullaby. The words are soothing sounds as in lullabies everywhere. Many Aborigine tribes sing their chants to the accompaniment of the *didgeridoo,* a wooden tube about four or five feet long. The player blows through one end like a trumpeter and by breathing in through his mouth can continue the droning sound of the *didgeridoo* for a long time. Singers also build exciting rhythm patterns by clapping their hands, slapping their bodies, or tapping wooden sticks together.

Traditional words   Traditional melody

Mum - ma   War - run - no   Mur - ra   Wa - thun - no

Mum - ma War - run - no   Mur - ra   Wa - thun - no   Mum - ma   War - run - no

Mur - ra   Wa - thun - no   Mum - ma   War - run - no   Mur - ra   Wa - thun - no.

Collected by H. O. Lethbridge

Jabbin Jabbin

The Aborigines who inhabited Australia before the arrival of the British lived close to nature, as many still do. This song imitates the birds waking at sunrise. One particularly noisy bird is the *gullah.* Another is the *kookaburrah,* known to generations of school children as the star of the round "Kookaburrah Sits in the Old Gum Tree."

Traditional words   Traditional melody

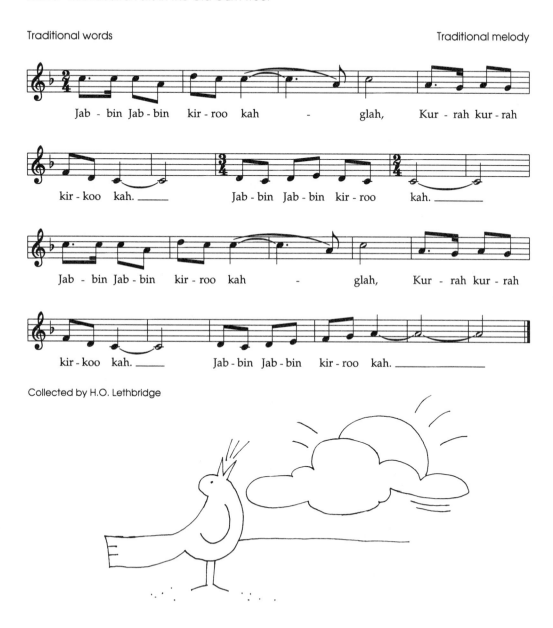

Jab - bin Jab - bin   kir - roo   kah   glah,   Kur - rah kur - rah

kir - koo   kah. ____   Jab - bin   Jab - bin   kir - roo   kah. ____

Jab - bin Jab - bin   kir - roo   kah   glah,   Kur - rah kur - rah

kir - koo   kah. ____   Jab - bin   Jab - bin   kir - roo   kah. _____

Collected by H.O. Lethbridge

Waltzing Matilda

This ballad tells the story of a *swagman* who carries everything he owns in a *swag* (a bundle) as he travels on foot about the countryside looking for work. A *matilda* was a kind of swag in which clothes and other belongings were tied in a blanket roll. He camps beside a *billabong* (little pond) under a *coolibah* (eucalyptus) tree. He steals a *jumbuck* (sheep) from a *squatter* (a settler on government-owned land) and escapes from the troopers by jumping into the *billabong*.

Words by A. B. Paterson

Music by Marie Cowan
Arranged by Allen Tuten

Chorus

Waltz - ing Ma - til - da Waltz - ing Ma - til - da You'll come a waltz - ing Ma - til - da with me. And he sang as he watched and __ wait - ed till his bil - ly boiled, You'll come a waltz - ing Ma - til - da with me.

2. Down came a jumbuck to drink at that billabong.
   Up jumped the swagman and grabbed him with glee.
   And he sang as he shoved that jumbuck in his tucker bag,
   You'll come a waltzing Matilda with me. *Chorus*

3. Up rode the squatter mounted on his thoroughbred.
   Down came the troopers one, two, three.
   Whose that jolly jumbuck you've got in your tucker bag,
   You'll come a waltzing Matilda with me. *Chorus*

4. Up jumped the swagman, sprang into the billabong,
   You'll never catch me alive, said he.
   And his ghost may be heard as you pass by that billabong,
   You'll come a waltzing Matilda with me. *Chorus*

Up in Space

This song was inspired by the words of American astronauts and former Soviet cosmonauts. After our travels around the world, it seems fitting to look at the whole earth from outer space and see what a small world we all have to share.

Words by Mary Lu Walker

Music by Mary Lu Walker
Arranged by Allen Tuten

Lyrics:

If ev-'ry-one could see the world from up in space. A lit-tle ball of green and blue, a love-ly place. No dot-ted lines a-cross its face, a home for all the hu-man race, it's

one small world._____ One world

One world One world love-ly place.

One world One world One small world._____

2. If everyone could see the world from way up high
   A little ball that's floating in a clear blue sky
   Then everyone could realize
   We share the earth, we share the skies
   Of one small world. *Chorus*

3. The forests and the rivers and the mighty seas
   The fishes and the animals, the birds and bees
   We'll take care of all of these
   And live in peace in harmony
   In one small world. *Chorus*

Bibliography

Andre, Evelyn. *Sing and Be Joyful*. Abingdon, 1979. Songs for young children, many of them with lyrics in other languages.

Challis, Evelyn. *Fun Songs, Rounds and Harmony*. Oak Publications, 1974. A nice collection that includes an international section.

Children's Songbook. Reader's Digest Association, 1985. A great collection with interesting arrangements of old and new favorites.

Cline, Dallas. *Homemade Instruments*. Oak Publications, 1976. Illustrated step-by-step instructions to more than 30 musical instruments, such as bongo drums and maracas, that children and adults can make together from easy-to-find materials.

Collins, Mitzie. *World Resonance, Cross Cultural Interpretations*. Sampler Records, Ltd., P.O. Box 19270, Rochester, NY 14619. A recording featuring rhythms and melodies from the West Indies, British Isles, and Middle East.

Haywood, Charles. *Folk Songs of the World*. John Day Co., 1966. Worth the search to find this amazing collection of the world's music.

Heritage Songbook. Holt, Rinehart and Winston, 1985. A little gem of a book containing 56 songs from around the world, most of them presented in English translations. Easy but inventive piano arrangements.

Rise Up Singing. Sing Out Publications, Box 5253, Bethlehem, PA 18015. Words and guitar chords to nearly 1,200 songs from near and far.

Serwadda, W. Moses. *Songs from Uganda*. Crowell, 1974. A beautifully illustrated book of songs with interpretation and notes by Hewitt Pantaleoni.

Smith, Robert J. *Here's Music*. Ministry of Education, Youth and Sport, Suva, Fiji. A paperback, which with its companion, *Vakatagi One*, is used in Fiji schools and not sold to the general public, but if you could wheedle, beg, or coerce the Ministry of Education into letting you have one you'd have a treasure because it's full of information about South Pacific Island cultures and their music. There's an excellent section on Indian music as well, since Fiji's population is almost half Indian.

Songs of Zion. Abingdon Press, 1981. A songbook from the traditions of the African American church. Excellent arrangements of over 200 traditional and modern pieces of church music.

Thomas, Edith Lovell. *The Whole World Singing.* Friendship Press, 1950. One of the first books published in America that featured international children's music.

Tucker, Judith Cook, with Abraham Kobena Adzinyah and Dumisani Maraire. *Let Your Voice Be Heard! Songs from Singing Cultures,* vol. 1. World Music Press, P.O. Box 2565, Danbury, CT 06813.

Warren, Fred. *The Music of Africa.* Prentice Hall, 1970.

Williams, Raymond. *The African Drum.* Highland Park College Press, 1973.

Some of these books may be out of print, but most are still on the shelves of public libraries. The Girl Scouts of the United States of America, 420 Fifth Avenue, New York, NY 10018, and World Around Songs, 20 Colbert's Creek Road, Burnsville, NC 28714, are good sources of multicultural materials.

Index by Title

Index by Country